CHICAGO'S RIVER
AT WORK AND AT PLAY

NEAL SAMORS & STEVEN DAHLMAN

Preface by The Honorable Richard M. Daley, Former Mayor, City of Chicago
Foreword by Lynn Osmond, President and CEO, Chicago Architecture Foundation
Introduction by Gary Johnson, President, Chicago History Museum

Chicago's River At Work And At Play

Edited by Neal Samors, Steven Dahlman,
and Jennifer Ebeling.
Produced by Neal Samors and Steven Dahlman.
Designed by Sam Silvio, Silvio Design, Inc.
Printed in Canada by Friesens Corporation.

For more information on this book
as well as authors' other works visit
www.chicagosbooks.com.
Email: NSamors@comcast.net or
news@marinacityonline.com.

Front cover
Trump International Hotel and
Tower from east on Chicago River,
Courtesy of Steven Dahlman.

Back cover
North Branch of the Chicago River,
looking north from Foster Avenue Bridge, 1952,
Betty Hulett, Photographer, Courtesy of
the Chicago History Museum, ICHi-68295.

ISBN: 978-0-9852733-5-4 (hard cover)
ISBN: 978-0-9852733-6-1 (soft cover)

To my wife, Freddi, daughter and son-in-law,
Jennifer and Michael, and granddaughter, Audrey.
Neal Samors

To my wife, Carol Pandak.
Steven Dahlman

The authors wish to express deep appreciation
to the following for the support and assistance they
provided in developing this book, including
excellent interviews and photographic materials.
Those individuals include:

Captain Robert L. Agra, Vice President, *Chicago's
First Lady*, Maurice Auriemma, General Manager,
35 East Wacker Drive Building, Simon Belisle, Program
Assistant, Great Lakes and St. Lawrence Cities Initiative,
David Clarkson, Sr. Vice President, Transwestern,
Nancy Cook, Docent, Chicago Architecture Foundation,
the Honorable Richard M. Daley, Janet Davies, ABC-7
TV, Gina Dorsey, TUR Partners, M. Allison Eisendrath,
Andrew W. Mellon Director of Collections, Chicago
History Museum, Margaret Frisbie, Executive Director,
Friends of the Chicago River, Rita Gaskins, Gary Johnson,
President, Chicago History Museum, U.S. District Court
Judge Charles Kocoras, Bill Kurtis, President, Kurtis
Productions, Christine Manninen, Communications/
GLIN Director, Great Lakes Commission, Jen Masengarb,
Director of Interpretation and Research, Bill Navarre,
Lawrence Okrent, Okrent Associates, Lynn Osmond,
President and CEO, Chicago Architecture Foundation,
Jackie Heard and Jodi Kawada Page, Katten Muchin
Rosenman LLP, Bobbi Pinkert, Docent, Chicago
Architecture Foundation, Philipp Posch, Hotel Manager,
Trump International Hotel and Tower Chicago, Robert
Prohaska, Director of Sales and Marketing, Trump
International Hotel and Tower Chicago, Dan Reynolds,
General Manager, Dick's Last Resort, Laura Saviano,
Marketing Principal, Ross Barney Architects, Billy Shelton,
Director of Merchandise and Product Development,
Chicago Architecture Foundation, Steve Shern,
Jeff Tigchelaar, David A. Ullrich, Executive Director,
Great Lakes and St. Lawrence Cities Initiative.
In addition, we want to thank the staffs at Hotel 71,
Merchandise Mart Properties, Inc., NAI Hiffman,
and the Renaissance Chicago Downtown Hotel
for their help in providing access to their properties
to take photographs of the Chicago River

Table of Contents

South Branch of Chicago River, photo taken from Holiday Inn Mart Plaza.

The Honorable Richard M. Daley
Former Mayor, City of Chicago

People from all over the world marvel at the beauty of Chicago's lakefront. But what is often overlooked is another body of water that is just as important to our city's history, identity and vitality—and its future: the Chicago River.

This river and the growth and prosperity of Chicago are inextricably linked. Our great city was founded on the banks of the Chicago River. It has played an integral role establishing Chicago as a center of commerce and transportation. And its reversal was not only a huge, internationally-recognized feat of civil engineering: it also symbolized our city's innovative spirit and ability to accomplish big things. In fact, the Chicago River is such an essential part of our city's history that it is symbolized as part of Chicago's flag.

I've always seen the Chicago River as a great asset to the City of Chicago and its residents. The restoration of the river and the ability of families and visitors to utilize it as a second shoreline was always a big priority to me during my time as mayor. Working together with advocates, businesses and civic organizations, we made a significant amount of progress cleaning up the river and reclaiming it for the people of Chicago.

For far too long the river was neglected. Its wildlife went unprotected. Its shores were damaged. The water was so deeply contaminated because of the decades of industrial waste that ran through it.

The Chicago River was a constant part of the neighborhood I grew up in. From the 1800s on, Bridgeport was where the immigrant workers lived when they were constructing the Illinois and Michigan Canal that connected Chicago to the Mississippi River. Growing up in the Hamburg section of Bridgeport, I have strong memories of Bubbly Creek, a part of the river that used to flow through the Union Stockyards where animal carcasses were discarded and methane gas from the decomposition would bubble out of it.

When my dad was mayor, he used to say that one day Chicagoans would be able to fish in the Chicago River. Of course, that statement was met by laughter from people because at the time the river was so polluted and its restoration seemed so unlikely. But he understood how the river connected so many neighborhoods and people as well as the potential that it had to be a natural and recreational resource to Chicagoans.

When I became mayor, I was determined to take the necessary steps to both restore and modernize the Chicago River. I've always said that Lake Michigan is part of the Chicago River and vice versa so we need to protect them both as a unit. Historically, since the reversal of the river, they've always been viewed as separate and we need to work as hard at protecting the river as we have with protecting the lake.

For years, the Chicago River was perceived as a boundary around Chicago's downtown area or Central Business District. One of my priorities as mayor was to grow our downtown and that meant new office buildings and other real estate needed to be developed on the other side of the river. This gave us a new opportunity to think creatively about how the Chicago River could fit within, and enhance our future plans. Shortly after I was elected to my first term, my administration partnered with Friends of the Chicago River, a local advocacy organization, to develop urban design guidelines for new riverfront development in downtown Chicago. The new guidelines helped to preserve and enhance the beauty and integrity of the river, while also expanding public access to the river for downtown workers, residents and tourists in ways that were not previously considered. Working together, we established Chicago as a national leader in reclaiming downtown waterways as assets. Other cities later followed our lead.

Over the next several years, my administration adopted riverfront design guidelines for the entire 28-mile length of the Chicago River, with the goal of making it a more valuable resource not just downtown, but for the many neighborhoods it runs through. Our 1999 Chicago River Corridor Development Plan and Design guidelines, along with a new citywide setback ordinance for riverfront development, set new standards for residential, commercial and industrial development, called for more public access and a continuous public trail system

These new guidelines generated a lot of new public attention for the Chicago River and led to new demand for riverfront development and recreational opportunities. Property values along the river, both downtown and in neighborhoods, increased and the river quickly became perceived as Chicago's second shoreline—a dramatic shift from its role from 100 years earlier as a sewer system.

Our progress on the Chicago River continued into the 21st century, when I directed the Chicago Park District to create a plan that would increase the amount of public open space along the river. Chicago's forefathers had the wisdom to create and maintain public open space along the Lake Michigan shoreline—a decision that helped maintain Chicago as one of the most beautiful, livable cities in the world—and I saw obvious benefits to Chicago's neighborhoods and residents from doing the same along the river. With the Park District's new Chicago River Master Plan as our guide, we began acquiring riverfront property and developing dozens of acres for new riverfront parks, while also creating new bike trails, walking paths and wildlife habitat.

With the Chicago River now a growing centerpiece of our city, beginning in 2003, my administration launched a renewed focus on water quality and conservation of the Chicago River, Lake Michigan and Chicago's other water resources. Many Chicagoans take water for granted because the city and region have been blessed with an abundance of fresh water resources. In fact, the Great Lakes overall represent 84% of North America's surface fresh water and 21% of the world's supply of surface fresh water.

But like other natural resources, there is a danger in their long-term sustainability without a plan to ensure their future. Without clean and plentiful water resources, Chicago's future as a city would certainly be in jeopardy.

So we developed the Chicago Water Agenda and the Chicago River Agenda, both of which laid out new, forward-thinking strategies for keeping our critically important water resources safe, clean and plentiful for future generations. Both the Water and River agendas were premised on my long-held and strong belief that government should lead by example. And both laid out aggressive new policies and programs for city government, with the goal of encouraging the private sector, civic leaders and residents to follow our models.

The city initiated a series of activities, including aggressive enforcement against illegal dumping along and into the Chicago River and removing combined sewer overflow outfall pipes along the river. While the Chicago Metropolitan Water Reclamation District's "Deep Tunnel" project became the primary long-term approach for dealing with storm water, my administration also issued new guidelines to promote innovative storm water management techniques. We launched programs to install French drains and permeable paving to enable water to be absorbed into the ground instead of sending it straight to the sewer system and increasing the risks of combined sewer overflows into our waterways. And we encouraged residents and businesses to disconnect their downspouts, use rain barrels, build green roofs and install more natural landscaping such as bio swales and native trees and plants.

We also pioneered the "ultimate disconnected downspout," when I charged the city and Park District to install a storm water management tunnel to capture clean rainwater from the immense flat roof of the new McCormick Place West convention center building so it could be diverted straight to Lake Michigan instead of going to the sewer system. The tunnel, which is 3,400 feet in length and extends from the roof to 160 feet below the surface of the lake, has the capacity to keep an average of 55 million gallons of water out of the sewer system every year.

One of the most exciting components of our river revitalization plan was the design and construction of the Chicago Riverwalk, which is located downtown along Wacker Drive on the river's main branch. The first phase of the Riverwalk was built into the design of the newly reconstructed Lower Wacker Drive, which opened in 2001-2002. The new East-West portion of Wacker Drive was built to accommodate a publicly-accessible walkway along the river's edge. This included connections under each bridge to provide a continuous walkway through downtown along the river, and space for retail, entertainment, dining and recreational activities. We completed the first phase of the downtown Riverwalk in 2005 with the opening of Vietnam Veterans Memorial Plaza, and the next phase was completed in 2009 which expanded river-level walkways beneath the Michigan and Wabash Bridges. This provided a continuous connection along the river from Lake Michigan to State Street. Residents can enjoy a closer connection to the river along with restaurants, cafes, water taxis, bike rentals, art exhibits and other attractions including the McCormick Bridgehouse and the Chicago River Museum.

Between 2005 and 2011, the Chicago Park District acquired more than 43 acres of new parkland along the river for parks and recreational purposes. The city built or expanded nine parks along the river, restored thousands of feet of riverbank, worked with the private sector to install more than 13 miles of riverwalk and adopted plans for several new canoe launches.

One of the things that people have to remember is that natural resources like air and water cross regional boundaries and, therefore, in order to take a comprehensive approach to conserving them, cities need to work together. Since they are connected, efforts we make in one area ultimately help many other areas. In 2003, I organized a bi-national coalition of mayors from the Great Lakes cities in the United States and Canada and formed the Great Lakes and St. Lawrence Cities Initiative (GLSLCI). The GLSLCI is an organization of local officials committed to working actively with federal, state and provincial governments to advance the protection and restoration of the Great Lakes and the St. Lawrence River. We began with only about 15 mayors. Over the years, the organization has grown to include more than 100 mayors and together we were able to deliver a strong voice to lobby for funding and ensure that these important resources are preserved for future generations.

By the time I retired from office in 2011, we had made great strides with revitalizing the Chicago River and it has clearly come to be known as a major urban destination. The architecture tours along the Chicago River are now one of the top 10 activities for tourists that visit the city. There are new boat launches up and down the river for motorized boats and for canoes, kayaks and row boats, both for sport and for pleasure. New parks along the river host neighborhood festivals, sporting events and other community activities. Additional bike trails and signage along the river direct recreational users to areas previously off limits or undiscovered, and many new species of wildlife can be seen all along and in the river.

I know the big strides we made to revitalize the Chicago River will continue. Yet future leaders will also have to deal with ongoing challenges such as keeping invasive species out, continuing to improve water quality, and whether or not the river should be re-reversed to improve the ecology of Lake Michigan.

Daniel Burnham in his *Plan for Chicago* envisioned public access to water as one of the keys to enhancing the city's quality of life. As a city, our goal has been to find innovative ways to appropriately combine the natural and built environments, such as the lake and the river, into a vibrant urban community for our residents. I'm proud to say, we have succeeded so far.

Too bad my dad isn't here to see it. Amazingly, the number of fish species in the Chicago River went from only 10 in 1974 to more than 70 today—and what do you know?—people are now fishing in it.

Lynn Osmond, Hon AIA

President and CEO, Chicago Architecture Foundation

How easily we forget that our river wasn't always so enjoyable. Today our guests gently float down the Chicago River, listening to a Chicago Architecture Foundation docent tell architectural stories, and capturing postcard-worthy images of the glass and steel skyscrapers to share with friends. It's hard to believe that this is the same river that William McCormick—in a circa 1860 letter to his brother Cyrus (19th century businessman and founder of what would become International Harvester)—described as "positively red with blood."

The mid-19th century river the McCormick family knew was primarily a working river—chocked full of grain elevators, swing bridges, and schooners ferrying lumber from the northern woods of Michigan. It also functioned as our city's sewer. Would the McCormicks recognize the Chicago River of today? Perhaps not. A typical summer afternoon finds our 21st century river filled with architecture river cruises, water taxis, tourists exploring the inner workings of a bascule bridge, kayakers watching fireworks, and office workers strolling along the river walk on their lunch break.

The Chicago Architecture Foundation (CAF), founded in 1966 by a group of Chicagoans who wanted to inform the public about the history of Chicago's architecture, created the concept of an architecture river cruise and launched their first tour to the public in 1982. Since then, CAF has been educating the public about the past, present, and future of the Chicago River and the important collection of buildings that line the water's edge. The mission of CAF is to inspire people to discover why design matters. For the past 30 years, the Chicago Architecture Foundation River Cruise, aboard *Chicago's First Lady*, has been an integral part of its educational portfolio of tours and experiences. Our volunteer docents interpret the architecture and provide an engaging narrative about the Chicago River and unlike any other experience in Chicago, the river cruise provides a unique perspective of the city and a three-dimensional timeline of key architectural periods.

For 90 minutes, guests are transported through a familiar, yet new landscape as a *Chicago's First Lady* boat navigates through the canyon of skyscrapers and bridges while CAF docents introduce key dates and events in Chicago history and the history of the river. The docents compare and contrast various architectural styles and explain the mechanics and history of Chicago's movable bridges. But more importantly, our docents give tour takers the visual literacy strategies to look closely at the buildings;

to take what they have seen along the Chicago River and then interpret structures and waterways in their own communities.

But float just beyond the shadows of the downtown Chicago's towering, glittering skyscrapers and the river takes on a completely different character. It's still a working river and one that the McCormicks would most certainly recognize. Although they operate at only a fraction of their 19th century levels, the retail, meat, grain, and lumber industries are all still alive in Chicago. The industrial sites used by these companies have left memories on the built landscape. These structures remain an integral, although altered, part of the city neighborhoods where they stand.

Like the city of Chicago itself, the story of our river has been one of development and growth, calamity and disaster, revitalization, and renewal. Historically, both city and river were seen as vacant, blank platforms for ingenuity and sheer will. The perfect example? Just after midnight on January 2, 1900, the Sanitary District of Chicago blew up a temporary dam—officially opening the Sanitary and Ship Canal and reversing the flow of the Chicago River. The canal was among the most important contributors to Chicago's prosperity, but it also led to challenges that we are grappling with today. It ensured public health by sending wastewater away from Lake Michigan, the city's source of drinking water, but it also forces us to send our most precious resource, fresh water, out of the Great Lakes watershed. It enabled economic wealth by allowing goods to pass between the Gulf of Mexico and Atlantic ports, but the interconnected system of waterways also provides a path for invasive species such as Asian carp to enter the Great Lakes.

A further challenge stems from the Chicago River's role as a piece of wastewater management infrastructure: keeping the river clean. The river is vastly cleaner today than it was several decades ago, thanks to water quality regulations and progress on projects to control flooding and divert raw sewage and runoff from the Chicago River. The river will become cleaner and healthier as Chicagoans' expectations of the Chicago River change.

The ecological challenges of this waterway will never be solved unless we also carefully address the infrastructure challenges of our cities. Many of the key issues Chicago continues to wrestle with surrounding water and its relationship to health, sanitation, manufacturing, commerce, service, and now recreation are the same issues that hundreds of other cities around the world face as well.

Our city has had a complicated relationship with the river. Over the past 400 years, we've tried to navigate it, defend it, profit from it, and control it. We've also abused and neglected this waterway. But the future holds a very different picture. Many of the new projects planned

12

envision the river's history as a catalyst for design strategies that might solve challenges facing Chicago neighborhoods and the region as a whole.

While Lake Michigan is certainly the region's greatest asset, Chicagoans hope the future of the river will bring new opportunities to enjoy our city's other waterfront. New boathouses along the north and south branches will become hotspots for kayakers, cyclists, and others looking for a place to play. Neighborhood riverfront trails will link parks. Planners and citizens imagined a renewed river edge in neighborhoods such as Pilsen and south Roscoe Village, where the riverfront is currently unwelcoming. Downtown, the banks of the main stem of the Chicago River are poised to become a civic promenade. In 2012, Mayor Rahm Emanuel announced plans to extend the Chicago Riverwalk from State to Lake Streets. And the Chicago River will continue to be the setting for iconic design, from office towers to residential high rises—inviting people to look out on spectacular views.

At work or at play, the Chicago River remains a powerful force of nature. Today the Chicago River increasingly mirrors regional goals to plan for and create a city that is more green, sustainable, and globally connected. Weaving together stories of past and present, *Chicago's River at Work and at Play* captures this shift and struggle. Neal Samors' deep historical knowledge of the region provides a new lens to view our city's evolving relationship with the river, and Steven Dahlman adds to the story with a series of magnificent photographs of the city's architecture as seen from the river. The Chicago Architecture Foundation is proud to be a part of this dialogue by continuing to engage the public through our river cruises, walking tours, bus tours, exhibitions, and public programs.

The Chicago Architecture Foundation is a nonprofit organization dedicated to inspiring people to discover why design matters. The Chicago Architecture Foundation presents a comprehensive program of tours, exhibitions, lectures, special events, and youth education activities, all designed to enhance the public's awareness and appreciation of Chicago's outstanding architectural legacy.

Chicago River by Gary T. Johnson
President, Chicago History Museum

Could it be that the word "re-reverse" is about to enter the dictionary?
The original 1900 reversal of the Chicago River stands as a great achievement
in engineering, but with the passage of time, and the passage of countless
gallons of Great Lakes water down the Mississippi River, reversing the
flow of the Chicago River may be an idea whose time has come and gone.
So said Richard M. Daley in 2008, when he raised that very possibility.

Of course, not every river could have been reversed in the first
place, even with engineering acumen. Certainly not the Amazon
and certainly not the Nile. But the Chicago River is not that kind of river,
because it moves through very, very flat land.

The flatness of the surrounding land is the key to the Chicago River's
importance in history. Ask a canoeist, and you will hear about back-breaking
portages over rugged terrain. Throw in a continental divide, and you can
imagine a particularly difficult portage involving ascent and descent. That,
fortunately, was not the nature of the Chicago portage linking the valleys of
the Great Lakes system and the Mississippi River system due to the proximity
of the Chicago River to the Des Plaines River. Most of the distance across
this particular continental divide (the one on the Southwest Side of Chicago)
came in the form of a six-mile wide marsh that was called "Mud Lake."

The "portage" was not only flat, it was marshy to the point of
sometimes literally making a watery connection. Picture the two fingers
almost coming together in Michelangelo's painting, *The Last Judgment*.
To French explorers Père Marquette and Louis Jolliet in 1673, that was
how this portage must have seemed, almost miraculous in its ease and
in its implications, as these two great continental systems came so close
together that sometimes they literally touched.

The permanent link between the two river systems came in 1848
with the opening of the Illinois & Michigan Canal, which joined
the Chicago River not with Des Plaines River, but with the Illinois River.
The length of the canal is 96 miles from Chicago's Bridgeport neighborhood to LaSalle. This was a decisive event in Chicago's history, as the
municipality grew from being a fur trading center to an emporium that
traded many kinds of goods. The opening of the Illinois Central Railroad
in 1856 reinforced the geographical importance of Chicago.

Aside from being very flat, the Chicago River is very small. The
headwaters of the North Branch lie amid the close-in northern suburbs
of Glencoe, Deerfield, and Winnetka—maybe a 40-minute car ride

from the mouth of the river in downtown Chicago.

The South Branch has its headwaters near South Racine and West Pershing in Chicago. That's about 20 minutes by car to the mouth of the river, if it's not rush hour. The two branches come together at Wolf Point, forming the stem of the Chicago River, a stem that is only 1.5 miles long. The whole Chicago River system amounts to 156 miles, and that includes not only the river itself, but 52 miles of built waterways: the North Shore Channel, the Sanitary and Ship Canal, and the Calumet Sag Canal.

Chicagoans generally do not know their riverfront as well as they know their lakefront. There is no famous riverwalk, as there is, say, in San Antonio, though, once again, plans are being discussed for upgrading the riverside in downtown Chicago.

My own two favorite places on the river are unexpected views into very specific Chicago neighborhoods. The first is Chinatown's Ping Tom Memorial Park which is located on the South Branch and is owned by the Chicago Park District. It includes a pagoda-style pavilion and a garden, and, since 2013, a boathouse. Developing this park became an important priority for a community that remained knitted together, despite the building of the Dan Ryan Expressway. It often is the turn-around point for river tour boats.

My other favorite unexpected sight along the Chicago River is the view from the Wilson Avenue Bridge over the North Shore Channel. The surprise is that many of the homes along the river have their own docks. Take a look when the holiday lights are twinkling from the docks, and you will experience cognitive dissonance. Your mind might be saying, "Is this somewhere in Wisconsin?," but you will, in fact, be in two neighborhoods that are home to some of Chicago's finest bungalows. Ravenswood Manor lies to the west of the bridge, and Ravenswood Garden to the east. The bridge itself was build in 1913.

My happiest childhood memories along the river were shared with Chicagoans from 1904 to 1967 on visits to Riverview Park, at Western and Belmont. For 27 years as an adult, I rushed across river bridges twice a day on my way between the Metra station on Madison Street and the offices where I worked in the Loop. Rushing commuters do not devote much time for reflection, the days when a massive barge owned by the Material Service Corp. passed under the bridge were times to stop and take notice and think about how the Chicago River was linked to other waterways. This company, originally founded by Chicago's Crown family, was the leading distributor and producer of building materials in the Midwest. Sometimes, too, I would smile when I remembered my grandfather telling me that when he was a child, and the bridges swiveled, you never knew whether you would make it across because the bridge tenders did not always bother to give warning when the bridge was about to trap pedestrians on the bridge as it turned to let boats pass.

The Chicago River has been the scene of some astonishing events. Consider these dates:

November 3, 1863: A passing ship spooked cattle crossing the Rush Street Bridge. The animals stampeded into the river, causing great damage to the bridge. This sad story also is a reminder, that during the 19th century, the commercial waterfront was the river front.

October 8-10, 1871: The Great Chicago Fire leaped across the South Branch and the Main Channel of the Chicago River in its drive to the east and to the north.

January 2, 1900: Water from the Chicago River begins to fill the Sanitary and Ship Canal. The miracle of reversing the flow of the river is now official.

July 24, 1915: The steamship S.S. Eastland capsized into the Chicago River. 844 people died in a disaster that killed more than twice the number estimated to have died in the Great Chicago Fire (over 300). Many who died on the S.S. Eastland were Western Electric employees who were on an outing.

April 13, 1992: This was an event that I can remember myself—the Great Chicago Flood. A damaged wall in a tunnel beneath the north branch of the Chicago River opened a breach and some 250 million gallons of water poured into a network of utility tunnels. Basements and other underground structures flooded throughout the Loop. The city watched breathlessly as efforts were made to stem the flow. It was astonishing to see that the river itself looked the same as always, but the streets were filled with surreal arrays of emergency vehicles and construction equipment. Buildings and manhole covers sprouted hoses everywhere. At the time, my wife and I happened to be hosting a scholar visiting from the University of Oxford who was fascinated with every development. "The failure of infrastructure! Now we know what it looks like." I, personally, never hope to see the failure of infrastructure again.

And now, one more day in the story of the Chicago River: July 6, 1907. This is a day that you won't read about in the history books, but I wish I could have been along the river that day at Foster Avenue. Why?

A photograph has come down to me of my great-grandfather, Henry Traffley, leading a family group on a fishing excursion on that Saturday at that very spot. (It is odd, isn't it, that a house painter would wear a tie on an outing like this, but times then were different.) Had I been there with him, he could have shared his memories of the Great Chicago Fire, 36 years earlier. Whenever I look at that photo and I see the forest, it seems like a window on the river as the Pottawatomi must have known it and the French must have found it.

The book that you are about to read offers many windows on a river whose story has astonished the world and whose future remains an open question.

Johnson family photo, including Great Grandfather, Henry Traffley, leading a family group at Foster Avenue and the Chicago River on a fishing excursion on July 6, 1907. Courtesy of Gary Johnson.

Chapter 1
The Early Years

CHICAG

This drawing taken by George Davis, a well known resident of Chica
of the Chicag

WOLFS

The building on the left was a Tavern kept by Elijah Wenthworth,
on the right was the Miller House. Each of them being used, as nec
Residences. Except the Fort, they we

Published by RUFUS BLANCH

ENVIRONS
OF
CHICAGO.
1891.

Chicago in 1832, Lithograph of Wolf Point,
George Davis, Artist, Courtesy of the
Chicago History Museum, ICHi-05947.

N 1832.

thful landscape of the locality at the junction of the two branches
en called

POINT.

Scott made his headquarters during the Black Hawk War. That
ht require, for Sunday Services, School Houses, Taverns and private
nost notable buildings of the place.

71 Randolph Street, Chicago.

A TRIBUTE TO THE WORLD'S COLUMBIAN EXPOSITION.

POPULATION OF CHICAGO
FROM ITS INCORPORATION IN 1837 TO 1891.

YEAR.	POPULAT'N	YEAR.	POPULAT'N.
1837	4,170	1866	200,418
1840	4,479	1868	252,054
1843	7,580	1870	306,605
1845	12,088	1872	367,396
1846	14,169	1874	395,408
1847	16,859	1876	407,661
1848	20,023	1878	436,731
1849	23,047	1880	491,516
1850	29,963	1882	560,693
1852	59,130	1884	629,985
1855	80,000	1886	703,817
1856	84,113	1887	782,644
1860	109,206	1890	1,099,850
1862	138,186		
1864	169,353	ESTIMA	TED FOR
1865	178,492	1891	1,200,000

400,000,000 years ago – The area that would become Chicago, and even the Great Lakes, lay beneath tropical seas.

20,000 – 14,000 years ago – A mass of ice known as the Wisconsin Glacier covered the Chicago area and the Great Lakes.

14,000 – 10,000 years ago – The glacial period included what were known as the Glenwood stage and the Calumet stage as the Wisconsin Glacier withdrew north and left behind moraines, rivers, and lakes. During that time, Native American hunters arrived in the area and became the dominant cultures.

1673 – Louis Jolliet and Fr. Jacques Marquette become the first recorded Europeans to visit the Chicago River harbor and write about their discovery of the Chicago Portage. Marquette returned in 1674, camped for a few days near the mouth of the river, then moved on to the Chicago River-Des Plaines portage where he stayed through the winter of 1674-75. Beginning in 1696, Frenchmen began to settle along the river and they established La Mission de l'Ainge Gardien near the present day Merchandise Mart. After raids by Native Americans, the Mission was forced to close around 1702. The first non-native in the area may have been a trader named Guillory who had a trading post near Wolf Point around 1778.

1783 – The American Revolutionary War ended and title to the area that would include the Town of Chicago changed from being British territory to becoming part of the new United States.

1780s – Haitian-born farmer and fur trader, Jean Baptiste Pointe du Sable, considered to be the founder of Chicago, and the first permanent resident, established his house, farm, and hotel at the confluence of Lake Michigan and the Chicago River. He was followed in the area by groups of Europeans who settled near what is now downtown Chicago.

1794–1795 – The Treaty of Greenville was signed by General Anthony Wayne after the Battle of Fallen Timbers. A group of Native American tribes ceded to the United States a six-square-mile section of land located at the mouth of the Chicago River.

1803 – After the acquisition of the Louisiana Territory in 1803, Fort Dearborn was established at present day Michigan Avenue and Wacker Drive by Captain John Whistler. Whistler had brought 40 men to the settlement called Chicagou (named after the wild garlic plant growing in the area) and the fort was named after Henry Dearborn, then the United States Secretary of War. Many settlers and soldiers and their families settled in and near the fort, but after the War of 1812 there was a growing fear of an attack by Native Americans who had joined forces with the defeated British.

August, 1812 – Settlers trying to abandon Fort Dearborn (including 86 adults and 12 children) were killed during a Potawatomi uprising in what was one of the bloodiest events to occur in what would become Chicago. In addition, the fort was destroyed.

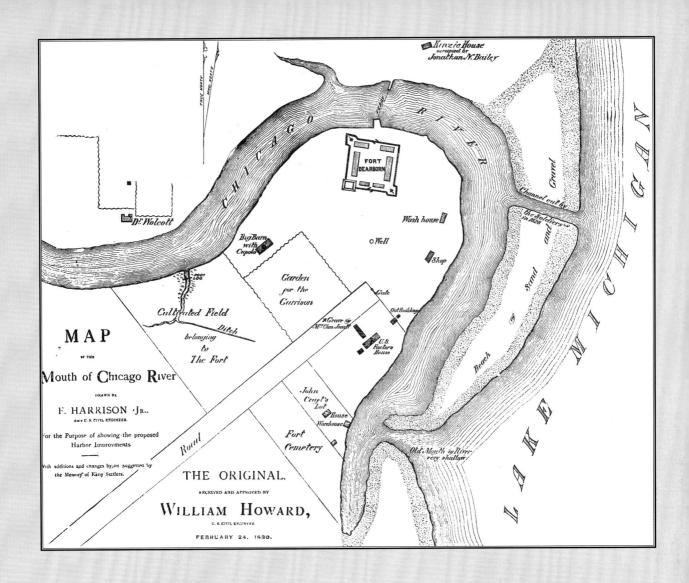

Map of Mouth of the Chicago River,
February 24, 1830, Drawn by F. Harrison Jr.,
Courtesy of the Chicago History Museum,
ICHi-21558.

Kinzie Mansion in 1833, Artist, Charles
E. Petford, Artist, Courtesy of the Chicago
History Museum, ICHi-01222.

Plaque on the Marquette Cross circa 1907,
Photographer, Charles R. Clark, Photographer,
Courtesy of the Chicago History Museum,
ICHi-68311.

Junction of the Chicago River, 1865,
Jevne & Almini, Creators, Courtesy of the
Chicago History Museum, ICHi-62075.

Rush Street Bridge and ship activity
on the Chicago River, 1866, Jevne and Almini,
Lithographers, Courtesy of the Chicago
History Museum, ICHi-63087.

1816 – A second Fort Dearborn was constructed on the site of the old fort. It became the center for military activity and during the Black Hawk War, area residents took refuge there. The second fort was decommissioned in 1837. (Parts of the fort were lost to the widening of the Chicago River in 1855 and, then, by a fire in 1857. The last vestiges of Fort Dearborn were destroyed by the Great Chicago Fire of October, 1871)

August 14, 1816 – Several Native American tribes signed the Treaty of St. Louis and ceded to the U.S. government a section of land that was 20 miles wide and 10 miles long on either side of the potential Illinois-Michigan Canal. The Indian Boundary Lines that resulted from the treaty were located to the south in Calumet and to the north which later became the towns and then the Chicago neighborhoods of West Ridge and Rogers Park.

1816–1828 – Soldiers from Fort Dearborn cut channels through the sandbar at the mouth of the river to allow yawls to bring supplies to the fort. However, those channels rapidly became clogged with sand which required new ones to be dug.

1818 – Illinois was admitted to the Union as the 18th state with a northern boundary at 42 degrees, 30 minutes north latitude that included the southwestern tip of Lake Michigan. Those boundaries included the entire proposed Illinois and Michigan Canal that would stretch from the lake westward to the Mississippi River.

August 29, 1821 – The Treaty of Chicago, signed by Michigan Territorial Governor Lewis Cass, Solomon Sibley for the United States, and representatives of the Ottawa, Ojibwe, and Potawatomi tribes, ceded to the United States all lands in the Michigan Territory south of the Grand River as well as a tract of land around the south end of Lake Michigan.

1832–1833 – After the defeat of Chief Blackhawk and his followers in the Blackhawk War of 1832, Native Americans from several tribes living in the region signed the second Treaty of Chicago which ceded their rights to any territory in Illinois to the United States government. As a result, the United Bands of Chippewa, Potawatomi, and Ottawa received cash payments and agreed to move to reservations further west, thus opening up the area around and including Chicago to white settlement. Land was subsequently purchased from the U.S. government for $1.25 an acre by settlers who moved into the region from the Midwest and East. In 1833, Chicago was incorporated as a town, and residents passed the first anti-pollution ordinance for the Chicago River.

1830s – Settlement began along the North Branch of the Chicago River north to what became Lake County. Early settlers named the North Branch the Guarie River, or Gary's River, after a trader who had settled on the west bank of the river a short distance from Wolf Point, at what is now Fulton Street. Guarie may have been the first non-indigenous settler at Wolf Point, the location of Chicago's first three taverns (one operated by John Kinzie in 1828), first hotel (Sauganash Hotel) and adjacent first drug store, first ferry (operated by Archibald Clibourn), first church (started by Rev. Jesse Walker in 1831), and first wooden bridge across the Chicago River (1832).

Boats in the Ogden Slip, n.d., Unknown Photographer, Courtesy of the Chicago History Museum, ICHi-68264.

Passenger ship *Christopher Columbus* docked at the Goodrich Docks, circa 1905, Barnes-Crosby, Photographer, Courtesy of the Chicago History Museum, ICHi-19159.

Rush Street Bridge and boats on the Chicago River, 1905, Unknown Photographer, Courtesy of the Chicago History Museum, ICHi-21621.

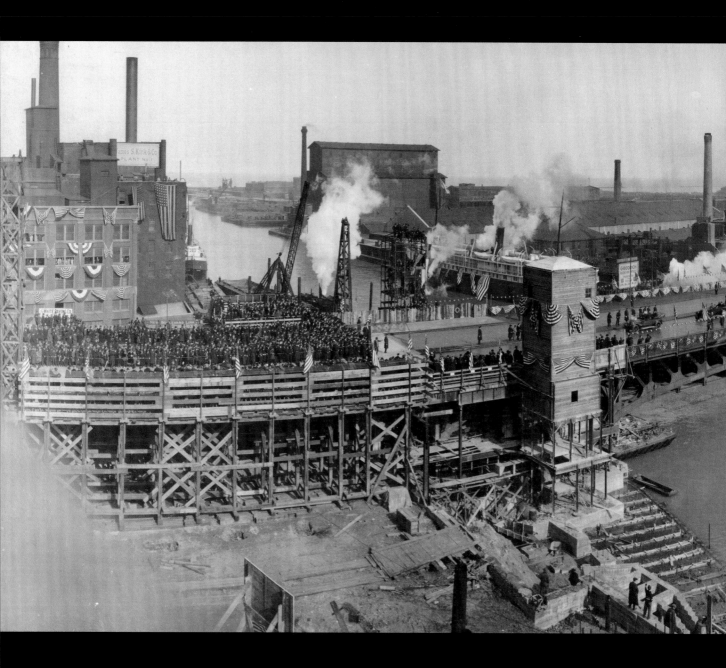

Panorama of Opening Day Parade and
Celebration on Michigan Avenue Bridge, May
14, 1920, Unknown Photographer, Courtesy of
the Chicago History Museum, ICH1-00144.

(Today, the source of the North Branch is located in the city's northern suburbs where its three principal tributaries include the Skokie River (East Fork), the Middle Fork that rises from Rondout, Illinois, and the West Fork that rises near Mettawa and flows southward through Bannockburn, Deerfield, and Northbrook before meeting the North Branch in Morton Grove. The North Branch then continues southward through Niles before entering Chicago near the intersection of Milwaukee Avenue and Devon Avenue.)

1832 – The first bridge across the Chicago River was constructed over the North Branch at present day Kinzie Street.

1833 – A second bridge was built over the South Branch near Randolph Street.

1834 – Chicago's first movable bridge across the Chicago River, which was made of logs, with a 60-foot removable center section, connected Dearborn Street to the north side of the river. (Today, the Chicago River has 38 movable bridges spanning it, down from a peak of 52 bridges which were of several different types, including trunnion bascule, Scherzer rolling lift, swing and vertical lift bridges.) During that year there was also a first attempt to solve the city's sanitation problem by digging a drainage ditch down State Street that emptied into the Chicago River.

April, 1837 – The City of Chicago was incorporated.

1842 – The Chicago City Hydraulic Company established a water distribution system with a pumping station and several thousand feet of wooden water pipes with an intake pipe for the system located 150 feet into Lake Michigan off Lake Street. Water was conveyed by means of a 25-horsepower steam-driven pump in a station at Michigan Avenue to an elevated wooden tank from which it flowed by gravity through wooden pipes beneath the streets. The City of Chicago purchased the company in 1852, and by the beginning of the Civil War in 1861, the Chicago Water System consisted of 600 feet of wooden intake pipes to the pumping station and then a distribution system made up of 95 miles of cast iron pipes and three elevated wrought iron reservoirs of 500,000 gallons each. The major challenge for the city's water system was that the Chicago River had become a cesspool of raw sewage that flowed into it and through the sewer system.

1853 – The Chicago Land Company, under William Ogden, Chicago's first mayor, bought title to land on the North Branch of the Chicago River and, within the decade, the excavation of clay created the North Branch Canal and Goose Island as a shortcut between Chicago and North Avenues for river travelers. In the late 1840s, Goose Island was on the city's fringes and a group of Irish immigrants began squatting on the island. They purportedly raised geese on the island which they served at Sunday dinners. But, the original island was dredged away by 1865 and a new channel was excavated northwards. By 1857, the channel had rejoined the river and formed a shortcut past the bend in the river. North Branch Channel became known as Ogden's Canal and the island that was created there was nicknamed Ogden's Channel. In 1891 some aldermen proposed making the official name of the new island, Goose Island.

View of the Chicago River, east from State Street Bridge, circa, 1889, Unknown Photographer, Courtesy of the Chicago History Museum, ICHi-68283.

Boats on the Chicago River, east from Wells Street, 1888, Burke & Koretke, Photographers, Courtesy of the Chicago History Museum, ICH1-03752.

Boat passing under the Canal Street Bridge, November 11, 1899, Unknown Photographer, Courtesy of the Chicago History Museum, ICHi-00133.

Pillsbury's warehouses along
the Chicago River, 1907, *Chicago
Daily News*, Inc. Photograph,
Courtesy of the Chicago History
Museum, DN-0008512.

State Street Bridge opening, circa 1905, Barnes-Crosby Company Photographer, Courtesy of the Chicago History Museum, ICHi-19005.

Chicago River and State Street Bridge, 1873, Lovejoy & Foster Photographer, Courtesy of the Chicago History Museum, ICHi00174.

Metropolitan L Bridge, November 9, 1899, Unknown Photographer, Courtesy of the Chicago History Museum, ICHi-00143.

The Binghamton passing Adams
Street Bridge, circa 1898-1916, Charles R.
Clark, Photographer, Courtesy of the
Chicago History Museum, ICHi-31903.

Goodrich Dock on the Chicago River,
June, 1915, Hornby & Freiberg Photographer,
Courtesy of the Chicago History Museum,
ICHi-24359

Chicago River frozen during winter, (n.d.),
Unknown Photographer, Courtesy of
the Chicago History Museum, ICHi-68287.

1856 – Chicago began a plan to raise the level of city streets by 8 to 10 feet above natural ground level to accommodate a plan for a sewer system. This led to an increase in the amount of waste discharged into the Chicago River because the river could not cleanse itself of the sewage due to the high level of Lake Michigan.

1865 – The Union Stockyards opened, but decomposing animal carcasses by the millions along with animal blood and offal was dumped into the Chicago River, along with metal-plating sludge from nearby factories. It caused methane gas to form on the river's surface, and thus the bubbling that continues to this day which led to the nickname of Bubbly Creek for the South Fork of the Chicago River's South Branch. That location marked the boundary between the neighborhoods of Bridgeport and McKinley Park. Bubbly Creek had originally been a wetland, and during the 19th Century, channels were dredged to increase the rate of flow into the Chicago River and dry out the area to increase the amount of habitable land.

1869 – Dr. John H. Rauch formally suggested the creation of a Chicago Park District which led to the establishment of Garfield, Humboldt, Jackson, and Washington Parks in the city. Then, in the late 1800s, the Municipal Science Club (later renamed the Special Park Commission), headed by Jens Jensen and Dwight H. Perkins, initiated a study of the remaining natural areas in Cook County. In 1904, they concluded that instead of acquiring just new space for parks, the beaches and bluffs along such places as Lake Michigan, the Skokie, North Chicago River Valley, the Des Plaines Valley, Salt Creek, Flag Creek, Palos Heights, the Blue Island Ridge and the Calumet River should be preserved for the benefit of the public. Around the same time, Henry Foreman, president of the Board of Commissioners of Cook County recommended the creation of the Outer Belt Park Commission whose purpose was "the creation and establishment of an outer belt of parks and boulevards, encircling the city of Chicago and embracing the Calumet and Des Plaines Rivers and the Skokie Marsh." This led to a law passed by the Illinois State Legislature which named the Forest Preserve Act of 1905.

1869 – Construction was completed on the present-day Chicago Avenue Pumping Station and the Chicago Water Tower which became the only downtown building to survive the Great Chicago Fire. By 1871, an underground tunnel was constructed to deliver water from an intake crib located two miles from the shoreline in Lake Michigan to the city.

1920 – The Michigan Avenue Bridge, the first double-deck trunnion-bascule bridge, was opened. It connected South Michigan Avenue with what was formerly a combination of Lincoln Parkway and Pine Street and would become North Michigan Avenue, also known as Boul Mich, and then the Magnificent Mile.

Men on a Chicago River Inspection
Trip, 1906, *Chicago Daily News*, Inc.,
Photograph, Courtesy of the Chicago
History Museum, DN-0050091.

Chapter 2

The Waterway Systems:Stems, Branches, Illinois/ Des Plaines River, Illinois and Michigan Canal, Sanitary and Ship Canal, and Cal-Sag Canal

Illinois and Michigan Canal Lock, 1912,
Chicago Daily News, Inc., Photograph,
Courtesy of the Chicago History Museum,
DN-0059411.

1836 - Samuel D. Lockwood, one of the first commissioners of the Illinois and Michigan Canal, received authorization to hire contractors to survey a route and construction began on the canal on July 4, 1836. However, the Panic of 1837 brought that construction to a halt.

April 16, 1848 – As Chicago grew, the Chicago River continued to flow sluggishly into Lake Michigan, causing sewage and other pollution to be poured into the city's clean water source. This contributed to several serious health problems, including an outbreak of typhoid fever.

1848 – The Illinois and Michigan Canal was finally opened by Chicago Mayor James Hutchinson Woodworth in 1848, and from 1848 to 1852, it was a popular passenger route. During that time much of the Chicago River's flow was diverted across the Chicago Portage into the new Illinois and Michigan Canal, which extended from the Bridgeport neighborhood on the Chicago River south to LaSalle-Peru on the Illinois River. It allowed boat transportation from the Great Lakes to the Mississippi River and the Gulf of Mexico. Over the years, the flow of the South Branch of the river was intermittently reversed. It was the first regional public work project which created a permanent, navigable waterway between the Atlantic Ocean and the Gulf of Mexico.

The canal allowed ships to use the Chicago River to get to the Illinois River. Those large ships meant that the City of Chicago needed to develop movable bridges which could be raised and lowered to also allow pedestrians and vehicles to cross back and forth over the Chicago River. However, because the heavy traffic on the river led to the need to raise the bridges so frequently, it resulted in many traffic backups at the bridges, and this led to Chicago constructing tunnels under the river. The canal was fed by the Des Plaines and Calumet Rivers and by the South Branch of the Chicago River through a lift wheel at Bridgeport. In 1848, the Galena and Chicago Union Railroad opened Chicago's first railroad depot at Wolf Point on the southwestern corner of Kinzie and Canal Streets.

However, use of the canal was reduced in volume by 1853 with the opening of the Chicago, Rock Island, and Pacific Railroad that ran parallel to the canal. The Illinois and Michigan Canal was later replaced in 1900 by the larger Chicago Sanitary and Ship Canal.

1871 – The deep-cut on the Illinois and Michigan Canal was completed and the rate of reversal of flow on the Main and South Branches of the river was increased.

1887 – The Illinois General Assembly, partly in response to concerns that arose from heavy rains and flooding that occurred in 1885 that posed a threat to the city's water supply, called for a law that would reverse the flow of the Chicago River. It required taking water from Lake Michigan and discharging it into the Mississippi River watershed.

Photograph of a painting of the Illinois and Michigan Canal by Edward S. Cameron, 1911, *Chicago Daily News*, Inc., Courtesy of the Chicago History Museum, DN-0009358.

Illinois and Michigan Canal, 1912, Stanley K. Faye, Photographer, Courtesy of the Chicago History Museum, ICHi-68297.

Illinois and Michigan Canal looking east
from California Avenue, September. 14, 1914,
Hallenbeck, Photographer, Courtesy of
the Chicago History Museum, ICHi-68298.

New drainage canal under construction at
Sag Bridge, 1912, *Chicago Daily News*, Inc.
Photographer, Courtesy of the Chicago
History Museum, DN-0059043.

Those voting in the negative are
Messrs. Blackwell, Brown, Butler, Daw-
on, Dubois, Elliott, Fithian, Gorden, Gre-
ory Hamlin, Henry, Hunt, Lincoln, Moore,
oss, Stuart, Smith, and Webb—18.
So the resolutions were adopted.

From the Chicago American.

SSAGE OF THE ILLINOIS AND MICHIGAN

CANAL BILL.

t is with feelings of no ordinary pleasure that
have received the intelligence of the passage of
Canal Bill. We were not a little surprized from
information previously received, at the large
orities in both houses, in its favor. The promi-
t features of the Bill, we understand, are the
owing: The Governor is authorized to nego-
e a loan on the credit of the State, not exceed
$500,000, to be required to be paid in instal-
ts, as in the progress of the work it shall be
ded. The stock to be created, is redeemable
e pleasure of the State after the year 1860.
the interest payable half yearly at the Bank
Illinois, or in the city of New York, out of the
l fund. The money thus loaned, the pre-
ms arising from a sale of the stock, the pro-
ds of the canal lands and town lots, and the
ies arising from the canal, are to constitute
nal fund to be used for *canal purposes*, and
no other, until the canal is completed. The
ernor and Senate are to appoint three com-
sioners, who form a board of commissioners:
of whom shall be the acting commissioner,
is charged with the general superintendence
e work; another, president of the board;
the other, Treasurer. The board has power
point a secretary. The acting commissioner
lowed a salary of $1200 per annum; and
ther two, three dollars per day, while neces-
y employed,—their commission to expire
he first Monday of January, 1837. They
be removed by the Governor for good cause.
re entering upon their duties, they are to be

Bridewell—a thing we su
sible in civilized commun

CHICAGO PRICES

CORRECTED WE

Salt	bbl
Flour and Meal—	
Super fine	bl
fine	
Buckwheat flour	
Indian meal	bu
Grain—	
Corn	bu
Oats	
Wheat	
Provisions—	
Beef fresh	
do salt mess	
do do prime	
Pork mess no. 1,	
" " no. 2,	
One hog	
primo	
Dried beef	
Hams smoked	
White fish	
Butter keg	
Lard	
Cheese	
White beans	bu
Potatoes	
Tallow	
Hides dry	
Candles box tallow	
Building Materials—	
Lumber ass'd 1000	
Shingles do	
Square timber, length	
Brick per 1000	
Stone	cor
Lime	bb
Wood	cor

Auction

TO THE LADI

THE subscriber begs lea
Ladies that he will se
tion, at his Room, South Wa
Garrison on Friday next the

TOLLS,
ESTABLISHED UPON THE
ILLINOIS AND MICHIGAN CANAL,
FOR THE YEAR 1857.

On Freight Boats, per mile, - - - - - - - - 2½ cents.
On Passenger Boats, per mile, - - - - - - - 3 do.
On each Passenger 8 years old and upwards, (60 lbs. baggage allowed free of toll,) per mile, 2 mills.
On the following articles, per 1,000 lbs. per mile, and in the same proportion for greater or lesser weight, the rates are as follows:

Article	Mills.	Article	Mills.	Article	Mills.	Article	Mills.
Ale,	5	Coke,	2	Lime, common,	3	Rye,	3
Agricultural Implements,	6	Clay,	1	Lime, hydraulic,	3	Salt, in sacks or bbls.,	3
Animals, (domestic,)	3	Eggs,	5	Lead, pipes, sheet, and roll,	4	Seeds,	4
Beef,	4	Flour,	4	Lead, pigs and bars,	1	Saleratus,	5
Beans,	3	Fruit, home,	4	Merchandise, including—		Soap,	5
Beer,	5	Fruit, foreign,	6	dry goods, groceries, hardware,		Sumach,	5
Bones, (rough,)	2	Fish,	4	cutlery, crockery, and glassware		Scales,	6
Butter,	5	Furniture, Household,	5	and all articles not specified,	5	Sugar,	5
Baggage,	5	Feathers,	8	Malt,	5	Stoves and hollow ware,	6
Beeswax,	4	Furs & Peltries, Buffalo		Molasses, in hhds. or bbls.,	5	Sleds and Sleighs,	5
Bacon,	3	and Deer skins,	8	Meal,	4	Shorts and screenings,	3
Brooms,	5	Grease,	4	Marble, wrought,	8	Ship stuff,	5
Broom Handles,	5	Glue,	5	Marble, unwrought,	5	Spikes,	4
Broom Corn,	3	Grindstones,	2	Mill Stones,	3	Starch,	5
Buhr Blocks,	3	Gypsum,	4	Machinery,	5	Shot,	5
Barley,	3	Glass and Glass ware,	6	Mechanics' tools,	5	Steel,	5
Buckwheat,	3	Hemp,	4	Nuts,	5	Spirits, except whisky,	5
Blooms,	5	Hides, dry,	6	Nails,	4	Staves,	2
Bran,	3	Hides, green,	4	Oats,	3	Sand and other earth,	1
Bark, Tanner's,	5	Horns and Tips,	4	Oil Cake,	4	Stone, cut and sawed,	5
Barrels, empty,	5	Hair,	5	Oil, Linseed and Corn,	5	Tallow,	5
Coffee,	5	Hops,	5	Oil, Lard,	5	Tar,	4
Cheese,	4	Hams,	4	Peas,	3	Tombstones, not marble,	6
Crackers,	5	Household furniture, ac-		Provisions, salt and fresh,	3	Trees, shrubs, and plants,	4
Cordage,	5	companied by and be-		Pork,	3	Tobacco, not manufactured,	3
Cotton, raw, in bales	3	longing to emigrants,	8	Pot and Pearl ashes,	5	Tobacco, manufactured,	5
Cotton yarn and batting,	5	Hay and Fodder,	4	Porter,	5	Tin plate,	5
Coopers' ware,	5	Heading,	3	Pumps,	5	Turpentine,	5
Carpenter & Joiners' work,	5	Hoops and materials for,	3	Potters' ware,	5	Varnish,	5
Carriages,	5	Hubs, boat knees, and bolts,	3	Pitch,	4	Vinegar,	5
Candles,	5	Iron, pig and scrap,	4	Potatoes & other vegetables,	3	Whisky and high wines,	5
Corn,	3	Iron, Railroad,	5	Paper,	6	Wool,	5
Cider,	5	Iron, wrought or cast,	5	Powder,	5	Wooden ware,	5
Clocks,	8	Ice,	1	Rags,	4	Wagons and other vehicles,	6
Charcoal,	2	Leather,	5	Rosin,	4	White Lead and paints,	5
Coal,	1	Lard,	5	Rosin,	4	Wheat,	5

On the following articles, toll per mile will be computed by number or measure:

On each 1000 feet of Lumber, per mile, - - 1½ cent. | On each 100 cubic feet same, in rafts, per mile, - 2 cts.
" " 1000 Siding, " " - - 6 mills. | " " 100 split Posts or fence Rails, " - 5
" " 1000 Lath or Shingles, " - - 2 " | " " cord of Wood for fuel, (from Lockport,) per mile, 1 "
" " 1000 Brick, " " - - 1 cent. | " " cubic yd., (27 cub. ft.) dress'd or dimension Stone, 6 mills
" " 100 cubic feet of Timber, hewed or round, if | " " undressed or rubble 3 "
transported in boats, per mile, " - 1 "

The weight of box, bag, crate, vessel, or thing in which any article may be contained, shall be added to the weight of the article
itself, and toll computed accordingly.

By order of the Board of Trustees,

CANAL OFFICE, Lockport, 1857.   **WILLIAM GOODING, Sec'y.**

☞ Wood transported from any point on the Canal below Lockport, will be subject to no additional charge, that is to say, the
rates per cord will be 30 cents from all points below Lockport to Bridgeport, or vice versa.

Children fishing at the Illinois and Michigan Canal, Channahon, IL, 1946, J. Sherwin Murphy, Photographer, Courtesy of the Chicago History Museum, ICHi-68299.

May 29, 1889 – The Illinois General Assembly passed the Sanitary District Enabling Act, and a referendum approving the formation on the Sanitary District of Chicago passed by an overwhelming margin. The purpose was to develop a solution to the polluted Chicago River and Lake Michigan. The new Sanitary District completed the hydrologic connection between the Great Lakes and the Mississippi River watershed in 1900 by reversing the flow of the Main Stem and South Branch of the Chicago River using a series of canal locks and increasing the flow from Lake Michigan that caused it to empty into the new Sanitary and Ship Canal. The goal was to carry away Chicago's increased sewage and meet commercial navigation needs. Also, over time, the District annexed contiguous areas, and in 1903 its two largest additions were the North Shore and Calumet areas.

September 3, 1892 – The Sanitary District of Chicago began construction of a diversion channel for the Des Plaines River between Summit and Lockport as well as the Sanitary and Ship Canal between Bridgeport and Lockport. The locks built near Lake Michigan and at Lockport diverted the flow of the North Branch, South Branch and Main Stem into the canal and to the Des Plaines River.

1900 – The Sanitary and Ship Canal, from South Damen Street to the town of Lockport, south of Joliet, opened. It meant that the flow in the Main Stem and South Branch, which carried pollutants away from Lake Michigan drinking water, were completely reversed so that the Chicago River flowed toward the Mississippi River watershed. It was a combination sanitary and ship canal that stretched for 28 miles long with a width of 202 feet and a depth of 24 feet and was the largest municipal project built in the United States at that time. It not only kept sewage out of the city's drinking supply, but it also flushed the filthy Chicago River by using the clean water from Lake Michigan. But, since the water from the lake only flowed into the Main Stem and South Branch, it did nothing to ameliorate the pollution in the North Branch.

1904–1907 – The North Branch of the Chicago River between Lawrence and Belmont Avenues was straightened to receive future discharge of sewage and lake water from the North Shore Channel.

1905–1908 – Lakefront intercepting sewers were built to stop sewage discharge into Lake Michigan.

Crowd of people aboard the *Juliet*, the
Sanitary District inspection boat, January 20,
1900, Unknown Photographer, Courtesy of
the Chicago History Museum, ICHi-14876.

1907–1910 – The North Shore Channel was a drainage canal that extended from Wilmette to just south of Foster Avenue in order to flush the sewage-filled North Branch of the Chicago River, and the completion of the eight-mile North Shore Channel diverted wastes from the northern suburbs into Lake Michigan. The principal goal of the channel was to supply additional flow to the Chicago River North Branch, but, it also helped to drain wet areas in Wilmette, Evanston, and neighboring communities like West Ridge. Also, a dam at the confluence of the North Shore Channel and the North Branch was built in 1910 and that sluice gate usually prevented the canal from draining out into Lake Michigan at Wilmette Harbor.

1909 – Daniel Burnham's Chicago Plan was introduced and it called for the individual owners of lakeshore and river properties to create a recreational corridor even though Burnham's urban vision had greatly been achieved for most of the lakefront where parkland already stretched to the south and north.

1911–1922 – The Cal-Sag Channel (Calumet-Saganashkee Channel) and controlling works at Blue Island were completed between 1911 and 1922, partially reversing the flow of the Little Calumet River. It was 16 miles long and served barge traffic in what was once an active zone of heavy industry in Chicago's far southern neighborhoods and adjacent suburbs. But, its construction added to a growing debate over the use of Lake Michigan water and Chicago's attempt to treat the river by dilution. A series of court suits from other Great Lakes states located upstream, including Minnesota, Pennsylvania, New York, and Michigan, complained that too much water was being diverted into the channel to clean the Chicago River. The Sanitary District was only allowed to continue diversions at a reduced rate and was required to complete construction of sewage treatment facilities along with the construction of locks at the mouth of the Chicago River in order to keep too much Lake Michigan water from pouring into the river.

1913–1918 – A comprehensive Forest Preserve District Act was passed by the Illinois Legislature, and, on November 3, 1914, the residents of Cook County voted in favor of establishing a forest preserve district with boundaries the same as Cook County. In 1916, the Illinois Supreme Court ruled that the Act was constitutional. It took until June 25, 1916 for the first 500 acres to be obtained, and by 1922, the District's land holdings had grown to 21,526 acres.

1921 – The Illinois Legislature passed the Lake Calumet Harbor Act which authorized Chicago to build a deep water port at Lake Calumet. Then, late that year, Chicago adopted the Van Vlissengen Plan that focused on commercial shipping and industrial development.

1928-1930 – The South Branch of the river was straightened between Polk and 18th Streets and moved one-quarter mile west to make room for a railroad terminal. Straightening of the South Branch was done mainly for purposes of transportation, but the side effect was to help beautify Chicago. The straightened channel of the South Branch was done by digging a new channel 850 feet west of Clark Street and filling the old river channel. The North Branch was also changed when the Forest Preserve District purchased 1,100 acres of land between Lake Avenue and County Line Road in order to construct the Skokie Lagoons.

1928 – The Sanitary District Commission opened the North Side Sewage Treatment Works in Skokie, thus discharging into the North Shore Channel all treated sewage originating from the Lake-Cook boundary to Fullerton Avenue.

1933 – The Illinois and Michigan Canal was officially closed.

1933 – The Civilian Conservation Corps (CCC) began work to transform the Skokie Marsh ("Big Wet Prairie") into the Skokie Lagoons. The marsh was partially drained by local farmers, thus creating a peat bog, but during spring floods, the marsh turned into a lake that inundated adjoining property and roads. Then, between 1933 and 1940, the Civilian Conservation Corps (CCC) implemented a plan to control the waters and create the Skokie Lagoons.

January 1, 1939 – Controlling works and a lock at the mouth of the Chicago River at Lake Michigan began operation in order to prevent reversals of the flow of the river into the lake while still allowing the passage of navigation.

1946 – Congress authorized the Calumet-Sag Project to facilitate barge traffic between Lake Michigan and the Illinois and Mississippi Rivers.

1951 - The Illinois General Assembly created the Chicago Regional Port District to oversee the development of the harbor and port as well as the establishment of an independent municipal corporation with title to approximately 1,500 acres of marshland at Lake Calumet.

1958 – The Calumet Harbor port opened and that was followed on June 26, 1959 with the dedication of the St. Lawrence Seaway.

1960-1965 – The O'Brien Lock and Dam was built, thus completely reversing the Calumet and Little Calumet Rivers, which led to emptying into the Sanitary and Ship Canal instead of Lake Michigan.

Old and new channel of the Chicago River's North Branch, circa 1902, Unknown Photographer, Courtesy of the Chicago History Museum, ICHi-68296.

Children wading in the Chicago River at 44th Avenue, 1902, Unknown Photographer, Courtesy of the Chicago History Museum, ICHi-39312.

Lower-North Branch of the Chicago River near Forest Glen, Illinois, 1902, Unknown Photographer, Courtesy of the Chicago History Museum, ICHi-39428.

1309 Sec.15 MAY 5 1899

Opening ceremonies of Chicago Sanitary
and Ship Canal, May 5, 1899, Unknown
Photographer, Courtesy of the Chicago
History Museum, ICHi-31511.

North Branch of the Chicago River, looking
north from Foster Avenue Bridge, 1952,
Betty Hulett, Photographer, Courtesy of the
Chicago History Museum, ICHi-68295.

Railroad tracks alongside the Chicago River
during a project to straighten the river, 1929,
Chicago Daily News, Inc., Photographer,
Courtesy of the Chicago History Museum,
DN-0089537.

Aerial view of 18th Street and the Chicago River, May 5, 1929, Chicago Aerial Survey Co., Photographer, Courtesy of the Chicago History Museum, ICHi-50103.

Aerial view of the Chicago River Straightening project, November 17, 1930, Chicago Aerial Survey Co., Photographer, Courtesy of the Chicago History Museum, ICHi-50102.

Tugboat Alabama maneuvering the ship *Sierra* in the Calumet River, June 26, 1960, Tom T. Pake, Photographer, Courtesy of the Chicago History Museum, ICHi-68303.

Chapter 3
The River at Work and at Play

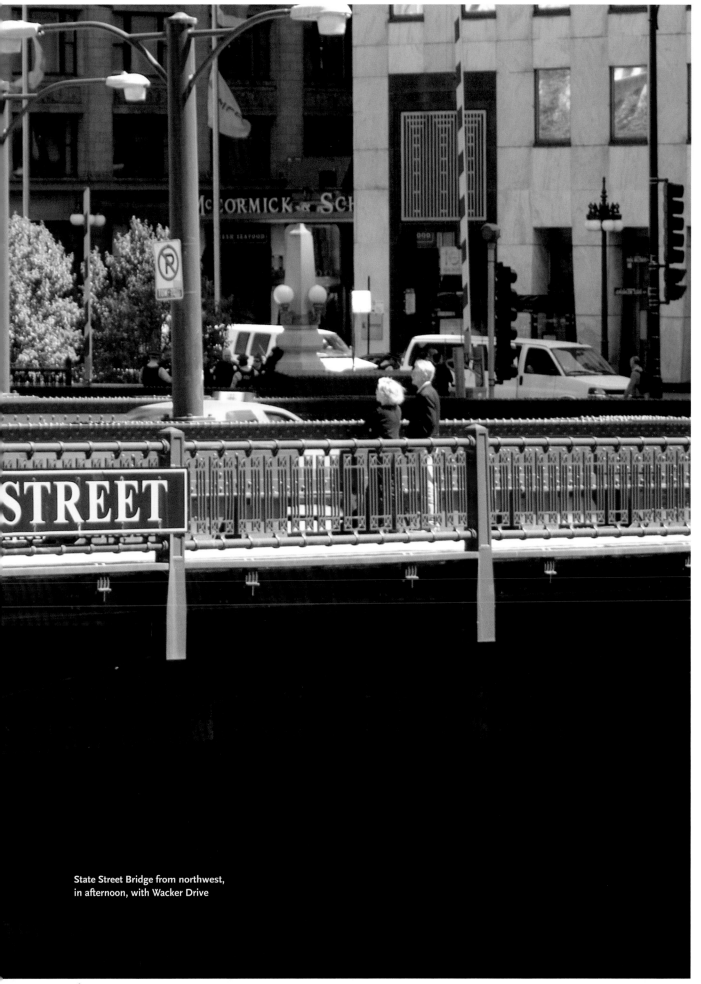

STREET

McCORMICK & SCH

**State Street Bridge from northwest,
in afternoon, with Wacker Drive**

Janet Davies
ABC-7

I think my first memory of the Chicago River was Bubbly Creek when I was working on an ABC-7 magazine show in the late 1980s called *WLS Presents*. We were showcasing the Chicago River and part of its legacy is Bubbly Creek where many of the old nearby slaughterhouses dumped their offal, manure, and carcasses. We traveled the creek in a canoe interviewing a naturalist who studied this part of the river. During the shoot we could plainly see the creek was still bubbling up years after the dumping ceased. I couldn't believe how many bubbles still popped the surface. We noticed regular river smells, but no methane or other gases from decomposition, which would have been the original cause of the bubbling.

In the middle of our interview a pair of Mallard ducks flew into the scene, landed on the creek and started paddling around. The naturalist became very excited. He claimed that although he was at that location almost daily he had never seen any ducks or wildlife using Bubbly Creek during his years of research. To him, it was a sign that the creek was making a remarkable comeback. We paddled along the riverbank in order to see if there were any birds' nests, another good sign. Our naturalist said he assumed there must be fish living in the water along with plant life below if the ducks were coming to the creek. How amazing is nature when it brings life back to a dead creek.

When I began my family, the river became more important. Over the years, I have paddled with them to the Skokie Lagoons for nice and quiet excursions. So many city and suburban neighborhoods have cleaned up their own areas along the river even putting in native plantings on the riverbanks. There is one neighborhood area that we particularly like between Irving Park and Montrose, and from the time my children were young we would go there, take bread, and make sure that the ducks were fed. One day I was with my oldest son, who was then about 8 years old, and we saw a fox on the opposite bank of the river. This city kid was so excited. Since then we occasionally see coyotes in our neighborhood that follow the river and wander off course. In fact, recently a pair of coyotes caused quite the traffic jam one morning while I was taking my youngest to school.

When Mayor Richard M. Daley was planning the river walk we continued to film several river walk-related stories. One of the more interesting tales was about a gondola tour that had been introduced on the river. The company used a couple of authentic looking gondolas but the tour only lasted for about one year. Perhaps with all the other boat traffic on the river, the gondola moved too slowly. And, the question of whether we really associate gondolas with Chicago helped hasten the demise of this idea. I know there are many wonderful ideas being developed from our Convention and Tourism folks concerning the Chicago River. It would be great to have a San Antonio type of river walk, but that is not possible. They have a smaller river on the city level and have developed it into a consumer-friendly corridor accessible by water taxi. We have a river that is below street level and used as a working waterway for all sorts of craft. We will reinvent with our own Chicago way of being creative.

One of my favorite city tours, and one I always take visitors on, is the Chicago Architecture River Cruise aboard *Chicago's First Lady*. The amount of city history that is covered on the tour never ceases to fascinate. Afterwards, I conduct my personal

Bubbly Creek at Morgan Street, circa 1911, *Chicago Daily News*, Inc., Photographer, Courtesy of the Chicago History Museum, DN-0056838.

Tugboat and passenger ferry on the Chicago River, 1830, Fred Tuckerman, Photographer, Courtesy of the Chicago History Museum, ICHi-68285.

tour because I am a history nut. We go to the spot of the Eastland Tragedy (I have produced manya story on this event). My captive audience is always amazed at the scope of this disaster while the steamer was tied to the shore! Then, we turn around and I point out the location of the docks and warehouses of Chicago's original commercial district, now gleaming high-rise office buildings. Over there is South Water Street, which was the site of the produce market that moved there after the Great Chicago Fire destroyed the riverfront.

In addition, Channel 7, located at State and Lake Streets, was the site of St. Mary of the Assumption in 1833, the first Catholic Church in Chicago. It was a wooden structure built at that site for the dockworkers working on the river.

The tour continues with the location of Fort Dearborn, explaining the why and how of reversing the flow of the river and the site where Chicago was flooded underground in the 1990's (Yes, I did many a waterlogged report during that crazy time). Also, answering the question—can you travel from the Atlantic Ocean all the way to the Gulf of Mexico with the Chicago River a part of that? And, yes, maybe we don't give this mighty river enough credit for the story of Chicago. It should take ALL the credit. If Jean Baptiste Point du Sable had not decided that this point of the river at the mouth of a great lake was NOT the best place to put a trading post, then we would never have become the City of the Big Shoulders, Hog Butcher for the World, City in a Garden, The Windy City, That Toddlin' Town, The City That Works, My Kind of Town, City on the Make, and The Jewel of the Midwest. And who else would dye a river brilliant green once a year?

Street scene on the Michigan Avenue Bridge,
1927, *Chicago Daily News*, Inc., Photographer,
Courtesy of the Chicago History Museum,
DN-0083157.

Michigan Avenue Bridge over the
Chicago River, July 20, 1970, Betty Hulett,
Photographer, Courtesy of the Chicago
History Museum, ICHi-68313.

Ogden Slip, looking west from the
Outer Drive Bridge, July, 1950, J. Johnson, Jr.,
Photographer, Courtesy of the
Chicago History Museum, ICHi-68289

Wolf Point area, March 14, 1951, J. Sherwin Murphy, Photographer, Courtesy of the Chicago History Museum, ICHi-23885.

Wacker Drive and the Chicago River, circa July 15, 1930, Chicago Evening American Photographer, Courtesy of the Chicago History Museum, ICHi-68288.

South Ashland Avenue Bridge, August 5, 1935, Unknown Photographer, Courtesy of the Chicago History Museum, ICHi-68293.

Launching of the *River and Harbor Patrol, Number 2*, 1912, Katherine McWeeney, Photographer, Courtesy of the Chicago History Museum, ICHi-24409.

Dredge Kewaunee passing under bascule bridges on the Chicago River, July 9, 1958, J. Johnson, Jr., Photographer, Courtesy of the Chicago History Museum, ICHi-68290.

Open elevated train bridge on the south branch of the Chicago River, July, 1960, Clarence W. Hines, Photographer, Courtesy of the Chicago History Museum, ICHi-68292.

Barges in the Santa Fe slip, July, 1949, Betty Hulett, Photographer, Courtesy of the Chicago History Museum, ICHi-68294.

Barges passing under the Madison Street Bridge on the Chicago River, 1929, *Chicago Daily News*, Inc. Photographer, Courtesy of the Chicago History Museum, DN-0089020.

Chicago River near Merchandise Mart, November, 1960, Edward F. Kloubec, Courtesy of the Chicago History Museum, ICHi-68305.

View of the Chicago River and surrounding
buildings at night, circa 1953-1983,
Hedrich-Blessing, Photographer, Courtesy
of the Chicago History Museum,
HB-SN-00825-B2.

Bill Kurtis
Kurtis Productions

I spent a lot of my life traveling the world and have learned that most cultures have a direct relationship with bodies of water found at those locations. For example, the river in San Antonio, which you could hardly call a river since it is more like a creek, has been lined with concrete so that shops and buildings can exist on it. It is a tourist attraction more than anything else and while people hear so much about their Riverwalk, the "river" is probably only 12' wide. In Oklahoma City, they have actually developed a river that looks a lot more like San Antonio, and there is a kind of restored area with an adjacent Old Town where there used to be brick buildings that served as warehouses. But, there is nothing around it and probably no more than a little mall with adjacent water. Other cities like Dallas and Omaha also have river walks.

As for Chicago, we have more potential for a river walk on the Chicago River than almost anybody in the country. First of all, it is controllable because the city's leaders decided to reverse the flow of the river to deal with serious sanitation problems in the 1800s. Second, it cuts through the heart of this major city, and I have not talked to anyone who has taken the architectural tour, while floating along on a boat, who hasn't rated that as Chicago's number one attraction they have experienced. They recognize that the river truly is the core location of the city's history.

Let me describe it as a journey that takes one both back and ahead in time. The past because it means everything since the 1800s since it is where Fort Dearborn was built and where the Great Chicago Fire jumped from the city's South to North sides. The river was where the main commerce took place for a hundred years with lake schooners and other ships docked along the river. And, in the 20th century, can you imagine going down to the river and watching the barges unloading rolls of pulp for the *Chicago Tribune* and the *Chicago Sun-Times* to use to print their papers? I actually rented a corner office in the Wrigley Building so that I could look down on the river and it was fantastic.

Then, there was the infamous S.S. Eastland disaster and the scientific achievement of reversing the river in order for citizens to be able to live healthier because fresh lake water poured into the river through the lock system and flushed the waterways. And, as you travel on the south branch of the river you go past Bridgeport where Irish immigrants first lived when they came to the country to help build the Illinois and Michigan Canal. There was also the issue of the vast amount of industrial waste, and the animal carcasses that were dumped into the river that are still bubbling up at Bubbly Point. It is also my understanding that the tall grass prairie could be found along the river at Mud Lake because when the French voyageurs came up the river they had to get into the water to their chests in mud and literally pull their boats along. There was also Portage Park which was the portage that travelers on the river had to make to continue up and downstream. From there west, there were no landmarks so the tall grass prairie with the big blue stems grew higher than everybody's head. It was not only frightening but difficult because you had to steer by the stars and the sun or simply lose your sense of direction.

It is important to note that Mayor Richard M. Daley had the vision and a plan for decades to clean up the river. And, the crowning achievement that no one seemed to blink at was a large bass contest. Everyone points to his father, Mayor Richard J. Daley,

Small ship passing under State Street Bridge, 1964, Calvin Hutchinson, Photographer, Courtesy of the Chicago History Museum, ICHi-39902.

who said that we would be able to fish in the Chicago River one day—and that has happened. The revelation to me was that during the flood in 1990 when river water poured into a forgotten underground tunnel, the divers who were going down the pipe to see about the crack at the bottom were checking on the break on and we could see it on television. Amazingly, there were fish swimming by and that was the first indication that the cleaning of the river was working.

Daley began the creation of a river walk and he handed the "torch" off to Mayor Rahm Emanuel. Rahm just recently unveiled a very aggressive $100 million plan for a longer river walk. One part of the plan is to continue the development of a river walk further east, north, and south, including a section beneath the Trump International Hotel, which is on the site of the old *Chicago Sun-Times* building. The river walk will continue for many blocks up and down the river. It was always the plan to be able to hike or walk along the river all the way from Chinatown on the south to Halsted Street on the north. Well, you can't do that today because the buildings still are built right up to the edge of the river. So, even if the city builds a walkway around them, there is still much to be done. And, the restaurants that were given licenses to set up shop along the river walk haven't had much success, except for some places like the Chicago Cut Steakhouse, with the best view of the river, and the Riverside Terrace, Cyrano's, and some hot dog stands. They are at least trying to draw Chicagoans and visitors to the city. But, they need business to survive and are doing some marketing and advertisements in local magazines to get people to use the river walk.

As to the future of the river, looking ahead, I do see a bright one because of the potential for further development along the river as a tourist destination. When my offices used to be on the 9th floor of the Wrigley Building, with a view of the river, the sound of jackhammers outside my office door was a little more than I could take. However, I looked straight down on the Leading Lady Boats, and, during the summer season, everyone was there and there were lines of people in front of our building. The foot traffic over the Michigan Avenue/Du Sable Bridge was fantastic, and it was truly the core and heart of the city. In the next 10-20 years, more people will have access to the river, including those who take the architectural tours. Then you have the kayakers moving up and down the river in a swarm because, during the summer they all come out at once. And, I almost was looking for swimmers to jump off the bridge like the kids do out in the countryside.

Just like the Daley Plaza with its Picasso statue, the river can become even more of a draw for people to visit the Loop. I can envision the river as being an extension of that center of the city for tourists, since now you can begin at Millennium Park, walk up Michigan Avenue, cross the Michigan Avenue Bridge, and continue down the Boul Mich/the Magnificent Mile as a wonderful stroll. All you have to do is walk and you don't have to spend any money at all. Then, if you can move by foot up and down the river and look up at the skyscrapers and stop for refreshments or even a full dinner, it will become the best way to see the city and you will realize what a bright future is ahead for Chicago. I think that we will be able to gather in Grant Park for the Fourth of July, visit the Taste of Chicago, and then go to a river festival, all in one day.

A variety of boats on the Chicago River shortly after it was turned green for St. Patrick's Day celebrations. Du Sable Bridge is in the lower frame and Wacker Drive is to the right.

Patio at Marina City's
Dick's Last Resort.

2010 Bank of America Marathon. Crowds
line both sides of State Street, seen
here from the Chicago Skyline Terrace at the
Renaissance Chicago Downtown Hotel.

Reflected in nearby windows, a variety of planned explosions rock the set of *Transformers 3*.

Important Architecture Along the River as Seen on the Chicago Architecture Foundation's River Cruise aboard *Chicago's First Lady*

Montgomery Ward Building from the
Chicago Avenue Bridge in late afternoon.

Bob Agra, *Chicago's First Lady*

We began our boat touring company in the 1930s as a family-owned business and I am the third generation. My grandfather originally started out at Navy Pier in the mid-1930s with a six-passenger speedboat and over the years the business has grown in number of boats, sophistication, number of employees, and scope of touring products. We have adapted to changes in the market in order to make the company a success.

In the early 1990s, we decided that the business was changing and that we wanted to adapt to new opportunities. Our response was to build *Chicago's First Lady*, which was a larger boat than we had previously and it could also be used for private charters and parties. It was a higher level boat in comparison to what we had been operating previously. My wife, Holly, who is the president of the company, is in charge of the sales, marketing, and the governmental relations end of the business as well as being responsible for operations and finance.

A major thing happened in the mid-1990s when Holly established a partnership between our company and the Chicago Architecture Foundation. She worked out an agreement with them so that we would operate their river tours, and, ever since, it has worked very well. We first began doing three cruises a day for CAF and now we are up to 14 cruises on the weekends in the summer. We also extended our fleet over the years and the Architecture Foundation has expanded its operations, which has worked well for both of us. Thus, we have been able to showcase Chicago's architecture and provide tours to many people from the Chicago area and all over the world in the 20-plus years.

In terms of our future business, as time develops, we have boats that range from being two years old to those that are a bit older. Thus, we would like to retire our older equipment and replace them with more modern and versatile boats, and that would be a normal ongoing process. Like any business, and to paraphrase what Marshall Field once said, "Give the customer what she (or he) wants."

Our number of customers on the river cruise has increased over the years, but our business is very dependent on Chicago's changing weather conditions. People are always realizing that the river is someplace that they want to see. But like anything else, you have variations from year to year depending on the economy, and, especially with us, on the ever changing weather conditions. While we have been doing well, our hope is that the numbers will continue to grow, and, I think that the improvements that the city is doing in planning for the future will help increase ridership. We operate from the middle of April until the middle of November with our busiest months being basically June, July, August, and September. During the earlier and later months of the year we are more dependent on seasonal weather when ridership is reduced and the boats aren't as profitable. But it makes sense to offer tours which are available for the customers as they come to town. In the fall, we get a lot of international tourists, while, in the summer, riders are more likely to be from Chicago and across the country.

The best thing about the CAF docents is that each one is unique, which means that you can take a tour one day, and then take a tour on a another day from a different docent and get a new and varied perspective of the city's architecture. As to the river tour itself, the boats depart from our dock at Michigan Avenue and the river, head

Tribune Tower and Michigan Avenue from Wacker Drive near a bridgehouse on the south side of the Chicago River, with the Wrigley Building at the left.

Chicago's Leading Lady
tour boat on the Chicago River
near Wolf Point.

west to the central junction before going up the north branch to Chicago Avenue, and then turn to go on the south branch as far as Harrison Street around River City. After that the boat turns around, goes north to the junction and then east on the central branch to the locks at Lake Michigan before returning to its starting point at Michigan Avenue. It is a 90 minute tour which moves along at a slow enough speed to allow the docents, who are commentators from CAF, to basically describe the architectural aspects of all the major buildings in the downtown area that are viewable from the river. The interesting thing about it is that it gives the docents a chance to have their own particular view of things and be able to personalize their tour. Each docent provides his or her own passion with their descriptions of the buildings and that are both educational and architecturally-based.

We also have a tour that travels into Lake Michigan. Those are our Urban Adventure Cruises and are similar to tours that my family has been offering since the 1950s. The cruise is a combination river and lake sightseeing tour that provides a detailed presentation about the history of the city and the Chicago River lock as well as much information about different aspects of the city. This tour provides views of the city that can only be seen while on Lake Michigan. The passengers who take that informative tour receive a presentation by our own staff. In fact, I have done that tour myself for a long time since there wasn't as much river and lake traffic. However, as the river and the lakefront have become busier with other boats, our staff give the tour and I focus on driving the boat.

In terms of what I consider to be the key buildings along the river, those would include the 333 Wacker Building, which is the curved Nuveen Building located between Franklin and Lake, and is very popular because of the way it reflects the different colors of the river and the sky. Of course, Willis Tower (originally Sears Tower) and the Wrigley Building are popular, but the cruise gives the passengers a clear sense of the many different architectural styles along the river, or schools of architecture, so to speak. Basically it comes down to what style of architecture or particular "school" that you like. Overall, there is something for everybody's taste and interest in the Chicago schools of architecture, whether it is the Old Chicago School of architecture south of Lake Street, or the Trump Tower, the newest building along the river, or post-modernism, or beaux arts style like the Crain Chicago Building at 360 N. Michigan. There are a lot of different styles of architecture in the city for whatever interests you.

In my view, the most important elements and aspects of the Chicago River waterway system include the fact that Chicago is located here because the river is here and that made the city different from cities like Milwaukee or St. Louis or any of the other cities and towns along Lake Michigan. The river is what allowed Chicago to grow during the 1800s to what it is today, and it is interesting how the downtown changed from being an industrial center into a modern city. The river has changed over the years but it still gives Chicago its unique character. Unfortunately, most Chicagoans don't really appreciate the value of the river in the city's history. In its early days, the river was used primarily for commercial traffic and for moving materials needed by the city and its industries. And, as time went on, the river became more of a tourism draw for Chicago especially with the expansion of the Chicago River walk from the lakefront and Lake Shore Drive to State Street. The city is in the process of finishing plans to start construction in the next couple of years on the expansion of

333 W. Wacker reflects the setting sun. Willis Tower is in distance, Wacker Drive is at lower right. Photo taken from roof of Merchandise Mart.

the river walk from State Street all the way to Lake Street that will enhance and beautify the river. The river has really become a place for both tourists and residents of Chicago. The river has definitely become more of an asset to the city over time.

The river has changed in the 40 years that I have been there, and I can only imagine and by looking at pictures how it has changed in the last 100 years. I believe that the changes in the river have been positive, although, maybe from a manufacturing or an industrial standpoint, it hasn't. But one of the nicest things about the *Burnham Plan* was that its authors looked at the lakefront as only being developed for the residents and the visitors to Chicago. It has meant that the industrial section of the lakefront was refocused to the Calumet River area, except for certain sections along the river's North Branch and southwest of Ping Tom Park and toward the south branch of the river and into the Metropolitan Sanitary District canal that remain industrial. The whole downtown area is becoming more recreational and more of an aesthetically pleasing and living area of the city. Those changes are working out well and the future looks good for the river. But, like everything, money is the biggest problem and any project which involves improving and beautifying the river will require great financial support.

Nancy Cook
Chicago Architecture Foundation docent

If you think about it, an approach that focuses on historic periods in Chicago's architectural development rather than discussing only the individual dates when buildings were constructed is a good way to understand Chicago architecture vis-à-vis the Chicago River. Thinking of themes to explain the river are difficult because in Chicago we don't have a simple overarching view of what the river should look like. The river is absolutely magnificent the way it is. I love the dynamism of it and its energy, as well as the fact that on a bright sunny day one might witness a guy who is talking on his cell phone while dressed in a wet suit and steering his Skidoo. So, I appreciate both the variety and the messiness. In addition, there are such background themes that include how and why the city's buildings were constructed, why they were built at that particular point in Chicago's history, and how the number of floors were determined for each building. All those things are fascinating to me and I think about it all the time, although I just don't have the time to answer such questions doing the river cruise.

When the tour boat is returning to the dock, and we are going to the west, there is a panorama of buildings constructed in the 1920s, the 1960s, and then the very contemporary Trump Tower that leaves such a visual impact. Chicago architects and engineers contributed to the structural innovations and new architectural ideas you see along the river, even in those buildings which visitors can't see from the river. During the river tour, if I had the time, I would like to be able to talk in great detail about such buildings as John Hancock Center, 311 South Wacker, Willis, Trump and earlier buildings and explore the innovations that went into their construction. You can actually see the John Hancock Center from the river if it is not cloudy or foggy. The architect of that wonderful building was Bruce Graham of Skidmore Owings & Merrill and the structural engineer was Dr. Fazlur Khan.

Chicago Riverwalk with Wacker Drive at left and McCormick Bridgehouse at lower left.

96

Back in the early 1900s, there were only brick buildings along the river like 325 N. Wells (Exhibitors' Building) and the Reid-Murdoch (Whirlpool/Encyclopedia Britannica). If one goes north, there is the former North American Cold Storage Warehouse, a river loft building on the east side, and then the Montgomery Ward complex. So, really those terminal-warehouse structures were the most important as well as the Holabird and Roche Great Lakes Building at Lake Street. These buildings of the early 1900s reveal that things began to change in Chicago architecture after the 1871 Great Chicago Fire. But it is difficult on the river cruise to tell detailed stories about that period of Chicago history. In fact, until the 1920s, there weren't any new, significant structures built in the city until the Michigan Avenue Bridge (Du Sable Bridge) opened. Then you had the four, corner structures at Michigan and Wacker, including the Tribune Tower, Wrigley Building, 333 North Michigan and 360 North Michigan (London Guarantee Building) which led to the development of Michigan Avenue as "The Magnificent Mile." They were each interesting structures because all had interior steel. And, with this modern development, those buildings were covered with a revival style exterior. At this time in the city's history, architects were going back to the past and exploring how to emphasize tradition. Then, due to the impact of the Great Depression and World War II and for years afterward, there was little new construction in the Loop until the early 1960s. Completed in the 1970s are the buildings perpendicular to and surrounding the Hyatt Hotel in Illinois Center. These are the only two Mies buildings in Illinois Center; others were designed by his disciples. In the 1980s, the city removed the hairpin turns on Lake Shore Drive over the Lake Shore Drive/Roosevelt Bridge moving the lanes eastward and then reconfigured the northbound lanes of Lake Shore Drive to create the Museum Campus in the 1990s. I talk about buildings along South Wacker Drive that you can see beyond the river because I think that Wacker Drive along the South Branch is where commercial real estate is happening. The convex green building is 333 West Wacker that was built in 1983, and, then, there was a surge in construction of new buildings in the 1980s. The buildings at 191, 225, and 333 West Wacker were not done by Chicago architects, but by Kohn Pedersen Fox Associates of New York.

I see Chicago as being totally dictated by structure and the architects who came here and studied with Mies van der Rohe or followed his philosophies as taught at the school of architecture at I.I.T. (Illinois Institute of Technology) were part of or are still part of the architectural firm Skidmore Owings & Merrill (SOM). I believe that there has been an historical progression in thinking, and Chicago continues to be a worldwide center of architecture because of those in the profession who worked and studied here and because of their influence on structure. Lake Shore East development, part of Illinois Center, is a hodgepodge, but I love the idea of a sunken park and that the complex is located at a lower level than the streets around it. The one outstanding tower is designed by Jeanne Gang of Studio Gang which is really a Mies tower with balcony fins. The context of the development is great and carries on that pedestrian quality of the buildings located behind and south of Lake Point Tower built at the end of the 1960s and early 1970s. Much is made of the contrast between Illinois Center and River East, but I am not certain that anyone on the boat can really see that. There is more walking space and multi-use in River East, but its towers are as various as those in Illinois Center.

330 North Wabash as seen from the roof of 35 East Wacker, with State Street at the far left. At the right, Wabash Avenue, the Chicago River, and Trump International Hotel & Tower are seen.

Reid Murdoch Center,
across the Chicago River.

I was surprised to learn that our river's bridges probably won't exist for long because they have to be continuously rebuilt. The trunnion bascule bridge makes sense because there is no center post to interrupt the flow of river traffic. I love the Chinatown railroad bridge, and I really like the one at LaSalle Street that was in the movie, *The Road to Perdition*, as well as other ones that have interesting bridge houses. But the rest of the bridge houses aren't very interesting except for the sculpture decorated bridge houses at Michigan Avenue that tell the Chicago story. The South Branch of the river is at this point not as interesting as the main branch and the north branch. I open up the river tour to questions on the way back to the Main Branch after I have finished talking about the Boeing headquarters. I do point out the Fire Academy and tell the story about Mrs. O'Leary and talk about the railroads and how the consolidation of rail lines and stations has changed the look of Chicago. When we make the turn to return north on our return trip, we talk about Willis (formerly Sears) Tower and narrate the skyline. I start out on the right side of the Main Branch of the river so that I can discuss modernism first because that is really Chicago's claim to architectural fame on the river. The North Branch of the river is very interesting and the contrast between the kind of open feeling when you go north and the congestion on the south branch is great. I also talk about Chicago's first mayor, William B. Ogden, the city's first colorful and powerful mayor, especially when we get to Goose Island. On the way back to the main branch, on the north branch, I enjoy talking about the important things that happened chronologically, why the city is what it is, and why it is a world-class city.

Aerial view of the Chicago River in 1997
looking east from the Main Stem, including
the North and South Branches, toward
Lake Michigan. Courtesy of Lawrence Okrent.

North Michigan and London
Guarantee Building (right) from across
Wacker Drive on a foggy morning.

Looking past the Wabash Street bridge
toward Trump International Towers
and Hotel and the Wrigley building.

Bridgehouse at south end of Michigan Avenue Bridge over the Chicago River. Sculpture is *Defense and Regeneration*, created by Henry Hering.

The Chicago Architecture Foundation River Cruise
adapted from *A View from the River*

Main Branch

Four hundred years ago, the Chicago River and Lake Michigan facilitated travel and trade among Native Americans. In the mid-seventeenth century, French fur traders made their living from the waterways, the surrounding prairies, and the woods. When Father Jacques Marquette and Louis Jolliet explored the region in 1674, they recognized the river's potential to help connect the Atlantic Ocean, the Great Lakes, and the Gulf of Mexico. Settlers who arrived in the 1830s beheld a waterway vastly different from today's river. Some called it a stream; it was slow-moving, marshy, and emptied into Lake Michigan approximately one-half mile south of where it now empties. A sandbar blocked direct access to the river and made entry dangerous for boats. But builders transformed the river, lining it with timber retaining walls, docks, wharves, turnarounds, grain elevators, and warehouses. The river became a symbol the burgeoning city's agricultural, commercial, and industrial strength. It also became Chicago's sewer. The rise of railroads, the growth of Chicago as a business center, the 1909 Plan of Chicago, the extension of Michigan Avenue across the river in 1920, improved sewage treatment and storm-water control, the establishment of the Environmental Protection Agency in 1970, the rise of the postindustrial economy—these were all factors in the transformations of the Chicago River.

The Lake Locks Offer a Lesson in Infrastructure
Settlers built Chicago on swampy land. They dug pit toilets and shallow wells; they dumped animal waste into the streets. When it rained, every hole and depression— including the wells from which drinking water was drawn— became a pool of mud and sewage. Ditches running to the river helped drain water and waste, but the ditches became clogged. Because of typhus and cholera outbreaks, the city raised the entire street grade in the late 1850s to construct a sewer system that emptied directly into the river. The resulting pollution threatened the city's main source of potable water, an intake crib in Lake Michigan. To protect the lake and bring clean water into the river, engineers reversed the river's flow in 1900 and connected it to the Des Plaines River southwest of the city via a 28-mile canal. The canal was deeper than the river, which at its mouth was deeper than Lake Michigan. Gravity pulled clean water from the lake into the river and then into the canal—and away from the city.

At first the city did not regulate the quantity of water drawn from Lake Michigan. But nearby Great Lakes states put legal pressure on Chicago to limit diverted water. In 1930 the federal government forced Chicago to build a lock at the river's mouth, limiting lake water intake to about two billion gallons per day.

View of Chicago Architecture
Foundation tour boat,
Chicago's Little Lady on the
Chicago River.

View looking directly west down the Chicago River at sunset, photo taken from the roof of Hotel 71 on East Wacker Drive.

Navy Pier

Charles S. Frost: original design, 1916
Jerome R. Butler Jr.: restoration of east auditorium building, 1976
Benjamin Thompson & Associates; VOA Associates: major pier renovation, 1995

In his 1909 Plan of Chicago, Daniel Burnham proposed a modernized harbor facility with two recreational piers; only one pier was realized, north of the Main Branch. The structure, originally called Municipal Pier, included a cargo facility, warehouses, an auditorium, a streetcar line, a restaurant, and grand views of Lake Michigan. During World War I, the pier housed Red Cross and home defense offices, carrier pigeon stations, and a jail for draft dodgers. After the war, the pier's name was changed to honor veterans. Navy Pier's popularity peaked in the 1920s, but the Great Depression and new leisure options—like drive-ins and amusement parks—sped its decline as a public attraction in the 1930s. The navy leased the pier during World War II and trained more than 60,000 troops on site. To educate returning veterans, the University of Illinois converted the pier to a campus. In the 1970s Navy Pier's future was uncertain. A $200 million renovation in the 1990s added restaurants, a ballroom, stages, exhibition halls, IMAX and Shakespeare theaters, a Ferris wheel, and museums dedicated to stained glass and another dedicated to children.

Lake Point Tower Condominium

Schipporeit-Heinrich; Graham, Anderson, Probst & White, 1968

Just west of the pier, Lake Point Tower demands attention. Schipporeit-Heinrich apparently based the building's design on a 1921 sketch made by Ludwig Mies van der Rohe their former teacher and employer. Instead of the four wings called for in Mies's design, the architects gave the structure a Y shape in order to provide better views and ventilation, while reducing the impact of the wind. At the time of construction, Lake Point Tower's location was controversial. In 1836 Chicago's founding fathers had decreed that the city's lakefront was to be "public ground—a common to remain forever open, clear, and free of any buildings, or other obstruction whatever." This dictum was not strictly observed. In 1964 the city planning department reaffirmed the need to protect the lakefront from development, with the exception of land on both sides of the river's mouth—most of which was owned by Chicago Dock and Canal Trust. The exception was meant to encourage improved harbor and terminal facilities rather than residential development. But that same year the trust leased its land to a Texas-based company that began to erect a skyscraper. Subsequently the planning commission closed the loophole with an amendment that banned multistory buildings from the water's edge. But it was too late to halt construction of Lake Point Tower.

Lake Shore Drive Bridge over the Chicago River, with Lake Point Tower in the distance.

Chicago Marine Safety Station
near Navy Pier.

Lakeshore East

The Chandler
DeStefano & Partners; Loewenberg Architects, 2007

The Lancaster
Skidmore, Owings & Merrill; Loewenberg Architects, 2005

The Regatta
DeStefano & Partners; Loewenberg Architects, 2007

The Shoreham
Loewenberg Architects, 2005

Looking at Lakeshore East's numerous construction projects, one can hardly imagine this location as a former landfill. The development's motto—"Where the river meets the lake"—would not have been a selling point for a residential community in the early 1900s, given the condition of the river. Today many buildings celebrate their proximity to the water in design and concept. Residences such as the Regatta and the Shoreham feature tinted glass, curving balconies, and green spaces meant to harmonize with the Chicago River and Lake Michigan. Such touches distinguish the Lakeshore East buildings from the modernist skyscrapers of the Illinois Center, built immediately to the west.

Aqua
Studio Gang, 2009

Studio Gang's building, designed by founder and principal Jeanne Gang, has become one of the most talked about early 21st century buildings in the US. Her design was inspired by the layered rock formations surrounding Lake Michigan. Undulating lines of the balconies give the building an organic, fluid feel and formed by the irregularly shaped concrete floor slabs, which also reduce wind pressure. The multi-use building—containing a hotel, condos, and rental apartments—is located in Lakeshore East, one of Chicago's newest neighborhoods. The building has won national and international acclaim for its design.

Balconies on the east side of Aqua, with the Blue Shield Tower in the background.

View from the roof of west tower at Marina City, looking southeast in mid-afternoon, toward the Aqua. The Chicago River is at the lower left and Lake Michigan can be seen in the distance.

Aon Center
Edward Durrell Stone; Perkins & Will, 1973

The Aon Center is sometimes called "the building that was built twice." When first erected, the structure was sheathed in Italian Carrara marble—the same kind used by Michelangelo. Its 43,000panels, however, could not handle Chicago's temperature fluctuations, and they began to buckle. The owners replaced the marble with North Carolina granite at a cost of about $80 million, more than half of the original construction cost of $120 million. The scrapped marble—all 6,000 tons of it—had a second life as trinkets, trophies, and landscaping stone.

Wrigley Building

Graham, Anderson, Probst & White, 1921/1924

With the Michigan Avenue Bridge under construction, William Wrigley joined the efforts to expand Chicago's downtown business district north of the river. He hired one of the nation's most prestigious firms to design a glittering monument to Chicago—and to chewing gum. In response to the property's challenging trapezoidal shape, architect Charles G. Beersman erected two buildings linked by a sky bridge. The Wrigley Building was clad in six shades of terra cotta—from light gray to pale cream to stark white—accenting the skyscraper's impressive height. When completed, it was Chicago's tallest building. For a quarter, visitors could take an elevator to the tower observation deck for breathtaking views and a complimentary stick of Wrigley chewing gum.

Wrigley Building, headquarters of Wm. Wrigley, Jr. Company.

Tribune Tower

John Mead Howells and Raymond Hood, 1925

In 1922 the Tribune Company's owners announced a competition with a $50,000 prize. The quest? To design "the most beautiful and distinctive office building in the world." The winning entry was a tower with chamfered corners and recessed vertical ribbon windows. The Gothic crown and flying buttresses lent the building an air both imposing and refined. The Tribune Tower's most popular feature is its base, where 150 stone fragments are embedded in the exterior wall. At the request of Colonel Robert McCormick, the powerful head of the Tribune, journalists gathered fragments of historically significant buildings from around the world. The pieces came from sites and structures such as the Taj Mahal in India, the Great Wall of China, and the Alamo in Texas.

360 North Michigan

Alfred S. Alschuler, 1923
Lohan Associates, restoration, 2001

Alfred Alschuler designed 360 North Michigan to fit its polygonal lot. Its upper floors are twelve-sided. The building's Beaux-Arts design features Corinthian columns that flank the central arch and allegorical figures that depict Chicago's early history. The top three stories form a classical colonnade, which is topped by a small Greco-Roman temple. The building's original owner, shipping insurer London Guarantee and Accident Company, placed its headquarters near the busiest port in the world.

333 North Michigan

Holabird & Root, 1928

The Art Deco details, setbacks, and strong vertical lines of 333 North Michigan display the influence of Eliel Saarinen's second-place Tribune Tower competition entry. Its base is polished black and purple marble, and the rest of the building is clad in light limestone and sculpted terra cotta. The reliefs by Fred Torrey depict Native Americans, early traders, Marquette and Jolliet, and Chicago's settlers.

75 East Wacker
Riddle + Riddle, 1928

Cattle-car magnate Alonzo C. Mather commissioned Herbert Hugh Riddle to design an impressive skyscraper. Working within Chicago's 1923 zoning ordinance, Riddle pushed the building to its allowable height of 264feetand added a narrow tower. Towers were allowed under the zoning ordinance if they were unoccupied and took up no more than one-fourth of the building's footprint. Because the lot was just 65 feet wide and 100 feet deep, 75 East Wacker was Chicago's most slender skyscraper.

Wyndham Grand Chicago Riverfront
Milton Schwartz & Associates, 1958

Constructed as a businessman's hotel in the first wave of new construction in the Loop since the Depression, the Wyndham Grand (formerly Hotel 71) is characteristic of other modernist buildings built in the years after World War II. The alternating horizontal bands of blue-green glass and stainless steel panels clearly express the structure of the building. The glass at the base of the building provides a transparency at street level, giving this massive structure an air of weightlessness.

35 East Wacker
Giaver & Dinkelberg; Thielbar & Fugard, 1926

Originally called the Jeweler's Building, 35 East Wacker contained a wholesale jewelry market. To protect merchandise, buyers and sellers drove their cars into a basement elevator and were transported to their desired floor. This was not the most practical amenity, as car elevators required more maintenance than passenger elevators and eliminated valuable floor space. The elevator was dismantled after just fourteen years of service. The building's dome was once the Stratosphere Lounge, a legendary speakeasy that was rumored to be a favorite hangout of Al Capone. Today it houses the presentation gallery for the architectural firm of Helmut Jahn.

Trump International Hotel and Tower
Skidmore, Owings & Merrill, 2009

The 92-story Trump Tower was designed to complement its setting. Each of its setbacks relate to a nearby building. The first honors the top of the Wrigley Building; the second aligns with the roof of Marina City; and the third setback is at the height of 330 North Wabash. The Trump Tower's curved shape and silvery-blue stainless steel, aluminum, and glass curtain are intended to reflect the river's color and curvature. The design contrasts, however, with the Beaux-Arts elegance of the Wrigley Building and the stark modernism of Ludwig Mies van der Rohe's 330 North Wabash.

AMA Plaza
Office of Mies van der Rohe; C. F. Murphy Associates, 1973

Once known as the IBM Building, AMA Plaza was Ludwig Mies van der Rohe's last skyscraper in America. Its design embodies his architectural tenet of simplicity. Because of the building's proximity to the river and its location on the bend, the dark bronze facade seems to rise from the green water. Today the building contains offices and a hotel.

Marina City
Bertrand Goldberg, 1964

Marina City embodies Bertrand Goldberg's vision for the modern American metropolis. Believing that urban areas should be centers of "synergy, growth, and community," he faced two major challenges: the flight of the middle class to the suburbs and zoning ordinances that restricted mixed-use development. His eye was on the future, and with funding from the union of building janitors and elevator operators—who had an interest in urban growth—he convinced officials to ease zoning and laid out a city-within-a-city. When completed, Marina City consisted of two residential towers, an office building, a bowling alley, swimming pool, health club, restaurant, and stores.

Close angle of residential towers at Marina City, photo taken from the roof of 35 East Wacker with 353 North Clark in the background.

Leo Burnett Building
Kevin Roche/John Dinkeloo & Associates; Shaw & Associates, 1989

In keeping with postmodernism, which exploits traditional architectural conventions, the Burnett Building revives Chicago's turn-of-the-century commercial style. The structure features a tripartite facade, divided like a classical column's base, shaft, and capital. Whereas many modernist buildings boldly display their steel, this structure is clad in granite. The colonnade at the base is repeated on a smaller scale at the fifteenth floor, acknowledging its neighbor, 55 West Wacker.

United Building
DeStefano & Partners; Ricardo Bofill Arquitectura, 1992

The designers of the United Airlines Building took as their inspiration the classical column, a popular feature in buildings from the 1880s to early 1900s. The components of a classical column helped architects devise an aesthetic solution to high-rise architecture. Designing a building so that it resembled a column stressed verticality and provided a unified appearance. The "base" of the building is sheathed in white granite; the "shaft" draws the eye skyward with long vertical pilasters; and the "capital" features arched windows and a pediment reminiscent of ancient Greek temples.

View looking northeast from roof of west tower at Marina City. Upper floors and roof of east tower are at the right, and the John Hancock Center and Lake Michigan are seen in the distance at the left.

LaSalle-Wacker Building

Holabird & Root; Rebori, Wentworth, Dewey & McCormick, 1930

The Art Deco LaSalle-Wacker Building was built in the form of an H, which optimized access to light and air while maximizing floor space. Chicago's 1923 zoning ordinance required setbacks when buildings reached 264 feet. The north light court (the inner part of the H) is visible in the photograph. At the twenty third story, a tower rises another eighteen floors.

Builders Building

Graham, Anderson, Probst & White, 1927
Skidmore, Owings & Merrill, addition, 1986

This structure at 222 North LaSalle was intended as a showplace for the construction industry. The atrium served as an indoor exhibition space for product displays. When Skidmore, Owings & Merrill designed the western addition, they maintained the building's original proportions and composition. The four-story glass-sheathed penthouse that connects the two sides is a modernist touch.

Merchandise Mart

Graham, Anderson, Probst & White, 1930

Marshall Field and Company built the Merchandise Mart to centralize and modernize its wholesale merchandising, which was scattered in at least thirteen different Chicago warehouses. The enormous facility, over four million square feet of space, was the largest commercial building of its day. The Great Depression, however, forced Field's out of the wholesale market, and the $32 million investment stood half empty until it was purchased by Joseph P. Kennedy in 1945 for one-half of its original cost. The Mart's limestone streamlined Art Deco facade features recessed vertical bands of windows, counterpoints to the building's horizontal mass. The entry lobby features murals by Jules Guerin, the illustrator of Burnham's Plan of Chicago. In 1953 Kennedy created the Merchant's Hall of Fame along the river esplanade "to immortalize outstanding American merchants." These bronze busts include Marshall Field, Edward Albert Filene, George Huntington Hartford, Julius Rosenwald, John Wanamaker, Aaron Montgomery Ward, Franklin Winfield Woolworth, and Robert Elkington Wood.

333 West Wacker

Kohn Pedersen Fox Associates; Perkins & Will, 1983

The design of 333 West Wacker had a major impact on the river architecture of Chicago. The architects' appreciation of and consideration for the setting distinguished their building from the many glass-and-steel boxes erected along the river in the previous two decades. Kohn Pedersen Fox's work challenged other architects to respect the river. Instead of conforming to its lot, the curve of the facade complements the bend in the river. The tinted glass harmonizes with the water and changes with the sky. On the sides that face away from the river, porthole windows line the base, and decorative details reflect the city grid.

Merchandise Mart from Wacker Drive
across the Chicago River, with the Wells Street
Bridge in the foreground.

35 East Wacker Drive in late afternoon, the
photo taken from the roof of the Wrigley Building.
The South Tower of the Wrigley Building is
in the foreground at left along with Hotel 71
and the Unitrin Building is at the right.

225 West Wacker from across
the Chicago River with the Franklin
Street Bridge at the lower left.

NBC Tower from West Wacker Drive in early afternoon, with Chicago River in foreground. At left, Gleacher Center (University of Chicago).

55 West Wacker in late afternoon, photo taken from 19th floor of Marina City west tower parking ramp. Wacker Drive is in lower part of frame with Willis Tower seen in distance.

Kemper Building at Wacker Drive and State Street in early evening with 35 West Wacker Drive at left and The Wit Hotel at right.

North Branch

In Lake County, just north of Chicago, three forks meet to form the North Branch of the Chicago River. A mixed landscape of marshes and woods, the North Branch was much used in the 1830s for recreational activities such as swimming, ice skating, and fishing. While the North Branch did not play as much of a role in the industrial and commercial growth of Chicago as the South Branch or the Main Branch, early settlers deforested, drained, and ditched the adjacent lands to exploit the rich soil. A layer of ceramic tiles laid underground prevented fields from soaking up excess water, which ditches diverted to the river. Erosion and deforestation contributed to floods all along the North Branch; they frequently reached the downtown area. The many recent building conversion projects and residential developments demonstrate that the North Branch has become a desirable place to live. But a boat trip up the river still reveals a quiet, forest-like setting only a few miles from the metropolis.

Residences at RiverBend
DeStefano & Partners, 2002

The facade of Residences at RiverBend curves with the river's graceful arc. Working with a shallow lot, architect Robert Bistry eliminated the standard central hallway. Instead the corridors run along the west side of the building, and all units have a river view. The lowest levels are townhouses; above them is a garage. Elevators lift cars into the garage because the building is too narrow for a ramp.

Fulton House
Frank Abbott, 1908
Harry Weese & Associates, renovation, 1981

Fulton House was originally the American Cold Storage Warehouse, and its repurposing as a residential structure brought surprising challenges. To keep stored products cool, the concrete floors were up to two feet thick, the outer walls were four feet thick, and there were no windows. Rooms were lined with horsehair or cork and cooled by a combination of brine and ammonia that flowed through two-inch steel pipes set along the floors and walls. In 1979 architect Harry Weese converted the building to loft-style condominiums. It took eighteen months to defrost the structure and required about 500 semi trucks to haul away the insulation. Holes were punched through the walls to create windows and balconies. Weese, who had a love for water and sailing, included docks for residents with boats.

River Cottages from southeast on Chicago River.

The Residences at Riverbend, at right, from east, in early morning. Wacker Drive is at lower left and Chicago River and Wolf Point are at lower right.

River Cottages
Harry Weese & Associates, 1990

Illinois native Harry Weese rejected "square box" modernism, believing that only after seeing everything ever built could an architect establish a doctrine. Though he did not quite see everything, Weese's work does reflect his travels, experiences, and especially his nautical bent. His River Cottages were a culmination of his enthusiasm for boating and his desire to see the Chicago River cleaned and revitalized. On the site of Chicago's earliest railroad depot, Weese designed four townhouses that celebrate their riverside location. Their triangular accents represent ship sails; the round windows resemble portholes; and each unit has a private dock.

East Bank Club
Ezra Gordon—Jack M. Levin Associates, 1979

Compared to the River Cottages across the waterway, the East Bank Club is a reminder of widespread perceptions of the polluted and neglected river in the 1970s. The massive, unadorned concrete structure turns its back on the water. Today it is unlikely that a prestigious sports center and private health club would shut out a view of the Chicago River.

East Bank Club from Kinzie Street Bridge in late afternoon.

Chicago River near Wolf Point in fall.

Kinzie Park
Pappageorge/Haymes, mid-rise units and townhouses, 2000
Nagle Hartray Danker Kagan McKay Penney Architects, highrise, 2002

If the East Bank Club snubs the river, and the River Cottages mark an early desire for river residence, Kinzie Park exemplifies a revived enthusiasm for the river as a valuable natural asset and property enhancer. This gated community was built just after the city mandated that new construction had to allow access to the Riverwalk. If a nonresident pedestrian wants to enter the site, he must notify the attendant.

River Bank Lofts
Nimmons & Fellows, 1909

George Nimmons was one of the country's most sought-after industrial architects. This was due, in part, to the commission he won to design the Sears, Roebuck and Company's complex in downtown Chicago. He was also known for decorative details such as the horizontal courses and the terra-cotta corner accents still visible on the converted River Bank Lofts. These gave the utilitarian buildings distinct identities. Today River Bank Lofts is an excellent example of the numerous conversions of early-twentieth-century warehouses and industrial buildings taking place along the North Branch.

350 West Mart Center in early morning
from across Orleans Street. Tenants include
Chicago Sun-Times and Holiday Inn.

Erie on the Park from southwest,
Montgomery A. Ward Park
in lower frame.

East side of River Place condominiums
from east end of Chicago River. One River Place
on left and Two River Place at right, with
North Branch of Chicago River in foreground.

600 West Chicago Avenue
(original Montgomery Ward warehouse)
Schmidt, Garden& Martin, 1908

One River Place
(second Montgomery Ward warehouse)
Willis J. McCauley, 1930

The Montgomery
(high rise, Montgomery Ward corporate offices)
Minoru Yamasaki & Associates, 1972
Pappageorge/Haymes, renovation, 2004

Montgomery Ward was a successful Chicago-based mail-order business at the turn of the century. The company needed an enormous space to fill all types of orders—from clothes to dishes to prefabricated homes. The original warehouse, called the Montgomery Ward & Co. Catalog House, curved low along the river, its red brick spandrels emphasizing its horizontality. The design of the second warehouse highlighted verticality. Ward's 1972 corporate high rise was a deliberate departure from the rest of the buildings, a looming monolith that juts above its industrial predecessors. The second warehouse and the high rise have been converted to condominiums. One River Place, the original warehouse at 600 West Chicago Avenue, is now home to several major tech companies.

South Branch

Civic Opera
Building

The South Branch was once a clean creek alive with plants and animals. It originated at Mud Lake, which connected the Chicago and Des Plaines rivers during the wet season. To connect the two rivers permanently, engineers built the Illinois and Michigan Canal between 1836 and 1848. In the late nineteenth century, Chicago became the meatpacking capital of the country as trains delivered livestock to the Union Stock Yards on Chicago's South Side for sale, sorting, and slaughter. Because anti-pollution ordinances were irregularly enforced, a great deal of animal waste was dumped into the South Fork of the South Branch, which became known as Bubbly Creek. Here is the testimony of Ed Lace, a Chicagoan who grew up nearby: As the animal carcasses settled to the bottom it began to rot. Grease separated and rose to the surface. Bubbles of methane formed on the bed of the river and rose to the surface, which was coated with grease. Some of these bubbles were quite large and when they burst, a stink arose. There were many local names for this part of the river, most unprintable. With the construction of the Sanitary and Ship Canal and the decline of the stockyards, the South Branch began to flush itself and the South Fork was filled in. Today the downtown portion of the South Branch is home to some of the city's most prestigious companies, and its banks are lined with architecture that emphasizes Chicago's business and Chicago's waterways, 1830 financial might.

Opera House
Graham, Anderson, Probst & White, 1929

When utilities tycoon Samuel Insull, the "Prince of Electricity," commissioned a new opera building for Chicago, he wanted a facility that would bring music to the masses. The result was a design in the art deco armchair form, giving the building its nickname of "Insull's Throne." The entrance along Wacker Drive features musical instrument reliefs, a two-story portico, and a grand pedestrian walkway. To provide additional income and keep shows affordable, most of the building is multiuse rental space. The Lyric Opera Building (as it was originally called) opened to the public with Aïda just six days after the market crash that launched the Great Depression.

Willis Tower
Skidmore, Owings & Merrill, 1973, 1985
DeStefano & Partners, 1993

The distinctive silhouette of the Willis Tower is a result of its structural system. Originally named the Sears Tower for the Sears, Roebuck & Company, the 110-story building is the tallest on Chicago's skyline and stood as the tallest building in the world until 1998. Architect Bruce Graham and engineer Fazlur Kahn created an innovative system of nine bundled square tubes to give the building its distinctive profile as well as all-important wind bracing. Two tubes stop at the fifty-fifth floor; two end at the sixty-sixth floor; three stop at the ninetieth floor; and the remaining two rise to the top. On a clear day four states are visible from the observation deck.

Willis Tower
(Sears Tower)

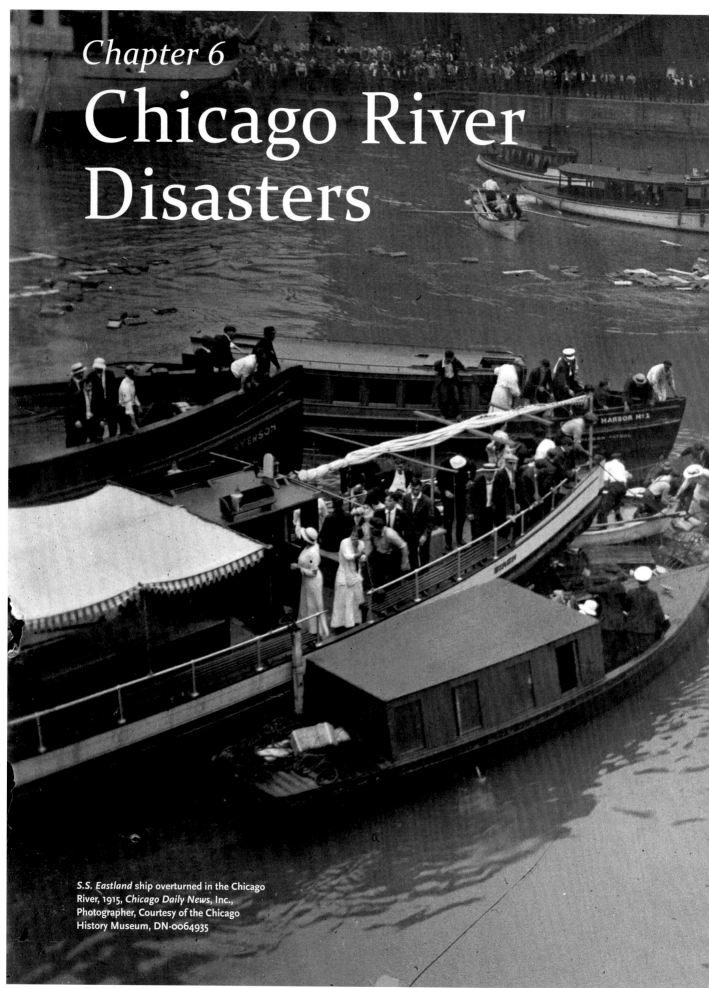

Chapter 6
Chicago River Disasters

S.S. Eastland ship overturned in the Chicago River, 1915, *Chicago Daily News*, Inc., Photographer, Courtesy of the Chicago History Museum, DN-0064935

1915 – On July 24, 1915, the *S.S. Eastland* was scheduled to take workers, families, and friends from the Western Electric Company of Cicero, Illinois on the company's annual picnic to be held in Michigan City, Indiana. Over 7,000 tickets were sold to picnic attendees, but the ship only loaded 2,500 people before raising the gangplank with the boat docked in the Chicago River. However, as the ship was getting ready to depart, the ship began listing to port and then to starboard, but did right itself. Then, the ship listed to port again as passengers rushed to one side of the ship and that led to the *S.S. Eastland* tipping over into the river. Many passengers were trapped below deck while others were forced to jump into the river. It became the single greatest tragedy in the history of the Chicago River or even the Great Lakes, and cost the lives of 844 people, including 22 entire families. Chicagoans responded by raising $350,000 for the relief of those families in need.

Survivors of the *S.S. Eastland* being led ashore by the tugboat *Kenosha*, 1915, Jun Fujita, Photographer, Courtesy of the Chicago History Museum, ICHi-30727.

The *S.S. Eastland* ship being righted after the Eastland Disaster, July 24, 1915, Jun Fujita, Photographer, Courtesy of the Chicago History Museum, ICHi-21067.

Eastland Disaster survivors and rescuers standing on hull of the steamer in the Chicago River, July 26, 1915, *Chicago Daily News*, Inc., Photographer, Courtesy of the Chicago History Museum, DN-0064944.

Eastland Disaster divers, circa July 24, 1915, Chicago Daily News, Inc., Photographer, Courtesy of the Chicago History Museum, DN-0064996.

Crowd standing behind police line on LaSalle Street during Eastland Disaster, circa July 24, 1915, *Chicago Daily News*, Inc., Photographer, Courtesy of the Chicago History Museum, DN-0064968.

Diver and men on a tugboat during the Eastland Disaster recovery efforts, circa August 28, 1915, *Chicago Daily News*, Inc., Photographer, Courtesy of the Chicago History Museum, DN-0065012.

April 13, 1992 – The Loop's Great Chicago Flood.

On the morning of April 13, 1992, 124 million gallons of Chicago River water poured through a crack in the wall of the river that had been caused when the Great Lakes Dredge and Dock Company mistakenly pushed a piling into the base of the river near the Kinzie Street Bridge. Work crews were unaware that, located beneath the river, there was an abandoned Chicago Tunnel Company tunnel that dated back to the earlier part of the 1900s. It had been used to transport coal and other goods, and although the piling did not break through the wall, enough pressure was created in the mud that it caused water to begin leaking into the tunnel. The resulting flood led to damage that totaled almost $1 billion by flooding buildings all across downtown Chicago including in the Daley Center, Chicago Board of Trade, Chicago Mercantile Exchange, City Hall and several department stores.

U.S. District Court Judge Charles Kocoras

Even as judges, we often get our news like everybody else. We learned about the Chicago River calamity in 1992 from the news media. The story was that a piling was driven into the wrong place in the river which proved to be the cause of enormous property damage. According to the facts alleged in a 1993 lawsuit filed by the city of Chicago against the Great Lakes Dredge and Dock Company, this is what happened:

"In December, 1990, the city invited marine firms, including Great Lakes, to bid on a project to replace 14 pile clusters, also known as timber dolphins, at five separate bridge sites in the Chicago River. Great Lakes won the contract. One of the sites included in the project was located at the south side of the Kinzie Street Bridge. During the last week of August and the first three weeks of September, 1991, Great Lakes' barge crew removed old, deteriorating pile clusters and drove new pilings into the riverbed at the Kinzie Street site. Over six months after Great Lakes completed its work under contract, on April 13, 1992, the Chicago River broke through the tunnel system running beneath the river and flooded Chicago's business district."

One lawsuit was filed in the United States District Court. Others were filed in the state courts. The federal suit was assigned to me and named both the city of Chicago and Great Lakes Dredge and Dock Company as defendants. Although there was limited personal injury claimed, there was extensive property damage to a number of downtown businesses.

Unbeknownst to most Chicagoans, there was a tunnel system running beneath the river that was once used to transport merchandise and other goods to department stores and other businesses in the loop. The flooding of the tunnel caused by the breach in the tunnel wall caused flooding in the basements and other floors of the businesses linked to the tunnel. Although there was insurance coverage for much of the damage, the insurance did not cover all of it. Even at that, the determination of fault had to be resolved, as was responsibility for each party's conduct.

One of the first issues to be decided was the one of greatest consequence to the outcome of the litigation. The question presented by the facts had to do with whether admiralty law governed the resolution of the issues—an exclusively federal process— or whether traditional tort law principles dictated the rights, obligations, and scope of relief for the injured parties. Admiralty and maritime law provide for a limitation of liability on the part of wrongdoers. The limitation on liability is the value of the vessel that caused the injuries or damage.

The vessels involved in the work being done on the river were barges. Workers from Great Lakes Dredge and Dock were using barges in a fixed position to pile drive timbers, also known as dolphins, in order to buttress or replace the existing timbers. The existing pilings were originally intended to protect a bridge contiguous to the pilings. The work and the pile drivings were being done based on maps of the area, and some of the fact questions to be decided were whether the maps were correct, whether the maps were correctly read, and whether the pilings were simply driven into the wrong place.

This was, for me, a difficult decision. As a federal judge for over 10 years to that point, I had made hundreds of decisions. The methodology I employ in disputed matters generally followed this path: read and understand all of the relevant facts necessary to the decision; research fully all decided cases bearing on the issue; and analyze the facts in the context of the applicable law. There is usually no set time by which the proper decision must be made. The issues to be decided must be internally thought about repeatedly and as long as necessary. At some point after exhaustive analysis, the conflicting choices sort themselves out and the strongest alternative settles in the pit of your stomach.

In this instance, and unlike most decisions I have made as a judge, I regularly vacillated between the two choices open to me. In the end, I decided that traditional tort law was the proper jurisdictional basis upon which the case should be resolved. In part, this is how my ruling read:

"In determining the jurisdictional issue between whether or not this is a maritime versus traditional tort law, it is as important to examine what the case does not involve as it is to examine what it does involve. First, none of the vessels were directly involved in the cause of the injury to the tunnel wall and did not strike anything to cause the harm in question; second, the vessels were acting as fixed platforms and were not involved in navigation on a waterway during the pile driving activities; third, the injuries were not sustained on a dock next to the work activities, but were experienced on land blocks away in Chicago's business district; fourth, pile driving is a common construction activity and is found in both maritime and non-maritime settings...the principal purpose of the placement of the timber dolphins at the Kinzie Street site was the protection of the bridge which the Supreme Court views as an extension of the land; fifth, the pile driving activities did not present a foreseeable or material destruction of maritime commerce on the Chicago River...the actual affect on commerce took place many months after the alleged wrongful acts and were part of the massive remediation efforts engaged in by the city and others; and, sixth, there are no allegations of personal injury on a vessel or on navigable waters, nor for damage done to a vessel in navigation or to its cargo."

It was my belief that it was the work on the river that was the significant event, which had little to do with navigation or commerce on the river itself. It was the pile driving of timbers making a hole in a tunnel that few people were aware existed. The Supreme Court of the United States had much less trouble than I did in determining that the admiralty law applied to the cases. Among other things, the Supreme Court held that the event did affect river traffic because of the temporary shutdown of navigation on the river and the necessity to make repairs. The Supreme Court vote was 7-0 with two justices abstaining.

Ultimately, the various disputes were settled by the parties and no trial was ever held.

The case was one of the most interesting disputes I have ever been assigned to for many reasons. The facts were quite novel and unlikely ever to be duplicated. The major legal question was whether admiralty and maritime law displaced common notions of fault and the award of damages commensurate with injuries. The sums of money at stake were substantial because of the ruination of much merchandise in the inventories of some of Chicago's largest department stores. The lawyers for the parties were excellent and taught me much that was new. The experience of presiding was as unique as the Chicago River itself.

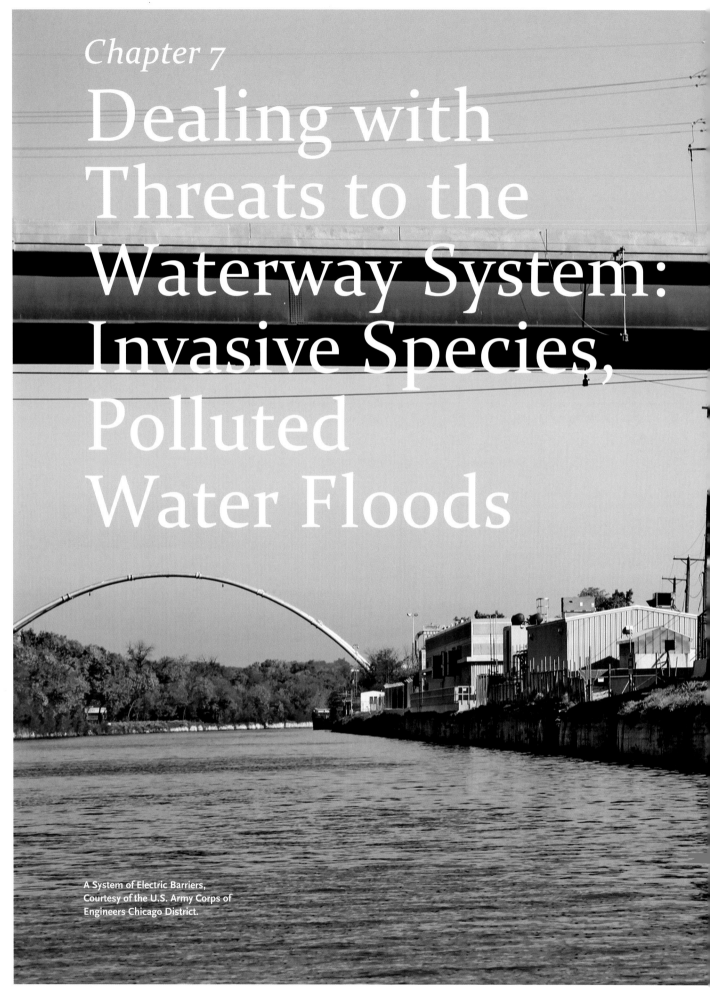

Chapter 7
Dealing with Threats to the Waterway System: Invasive Species, Polluted Water Floods

A System of Electric Barriers,
Courtesy of the U.S. Army Corps of
Engineers Chicago District.

David A. Ullrich

The Great Lakes and St. Lawrence Cities Initiative has a membership of over 100 U.S. and Canadian cities (70% Canadian and 30% U.S. cities), representing over 16 million people, and focus on both the Great Lakes and the St. Lawrence River. Thus, we have an interest in the issues that affect the rivers themselves, their many tributaries that feed into the Great Lakes, and the urban concentrations around them. Yet, for us, the Chicago River is unique and has been the focus of our attention for a long time. One of the most important reasons for our emphasis is because since around 1900 there has been a daily diversion of up to roughly 2 billion gallons of water from the Great Lakes into the Mississippi River watershed. I think this issue is a bit of a sore point with the rest of the Great Lakes area, particularly when there were discussions about the Great Lakes Compact between 2000 and 2008. The Illinois Diversion, as it is referred to (also sometimes called the Chicago Diversion), has a Consent Decree with the United States Supreme Court which controls the diversion. Basically the diversion has been "grandfathered" or exempted from the Compact so it can continue to be allowed under that decree.

A different issue came to our attention about 10-15 years ago with the movement of Asian carp up the Mississippi River watershed towards the Chicago River and the Great Lakes. As the carp got closer and closer to Lake Michigan through the Illinois River, people became more and more concerned because of the potential that they would get into to the Great Lakes. There is a long history of invasive species in our waters since over 180 different varieties of such species have already entered the Great Lakes. Many of these species have had devastating effects, including two of the most well known ones, the sea lamprey and the zebra mussel. But, many others have also had a dramatic effect. And, considering the kind of damage that the Asian carp were doing to the Mississippi River watershed, including the jumping ability of the silver carp, the broader public became more focused on this problem.

The federal and state governments have been working on this concern for some time. So far, the primary line of defense is an electric barrier near Romeoville that has been in place, to one degree or another, for around seven or eight years. It started with a demonstration barrier, and it is now more permanent. But, many people do not feel that this approach has been adequate and definitely not secure enough to stop the Asian carp from getting into the waterway system. The other element to consider is that it is pretty much a one-way electric barrier. And, what people don't often think about is that far more invasive species have traveled from the Great Lakes to the Mississippi River rather than the other direction. In addition, while the electric barrier may work with fish of a medium and larger size, a concern remains that smaller fish and species like mollusks and plants will not be stopped by this barrier. The U.S. Army Corps of Engineers has documented 39 different invasive species, including 19 on the Great Lakes side and ten on the Mississippi River side, that now, or in the near future, present a real threat to our waterways.

It was the combination of all of these threats that led our organization and the Great Lakes Commission in Ann Arbor, Michigan to argue that something more needed to happen, and at a faster pace, in order to deal with this problem. A conference that Mayor Richard M. Daley sponsored in 2003 that looked at invasive species and, specifically, the Asian carp and the Chicago River situation, had people talking about the idea of creating a physical separation in the Chicago Waterway System, and, possibly a re-reversal of some portion of the Chicago River back into Lake Michigan.

This concept of physical separation has been actively discussed since 2003, but it didn't seem to be taken very seriously. Since a lot of people were skeptical about this proposed solution, the Great Lakes Commission and our organization met with The Joyce Foundation in Chicago as well as a group of five other funding agencies. We said to them, "Listen, we don't think that the pace at which the federal and state governments are facing this issue is quick enough and we are concerned that they are not seriously considering physical separation as a feasible approach. So, we think that a better way to go about this is to do it ourselves by retaining an engineering firm and scoping out whether or not this is feasible." We were able to convince a group of these funding agencies to come up with $2 million to do an expedited feasibility study to explore whether or not a physical separation could be accomplished. Interestingly enough, the Natural Resources Defense Council, through their Midwest Office in Chicago, did some preliminary work on this solution with Shaw Engineering and also contracted with Jeanne Gang, the architect and author of *Reverse Effect*. In addition, the architectural firm of Skidmore, Owings, & Merrill has done a little work on this through famed architect Phil Enquist.

We began to focus our attention on the feasibility of this project and brought in the engineering firm of HDR to begin work in earnest in January, 2011 by laying out possible locations for barriers. HDR completed a study of the 130-mile system made up mostly of man-made barriers and together we decided to look primarily at Northeast Illinois and Northwest Indiana because the Grand Calumet and Little Calumet Rivers are part of this whole system. There were five potential locations where the Asian carp could get into Lake Michigan. We decided to look at roughly 20 locations where barriers could be placed. We discussed them at some length as to the advantages and disadvantages, and essentially developed three options. The first was a single barrier, which became the Down River Option, The second was a system of four barriers which we called the Mid-System which included four sites, including on the river's main stem, one on the Calumet River and two in Northwest Indiana. The third was the Near Lake Option, which includes five barriers on or very near the lakeshore. These would be full physical barriers with concrete sheet pilings, soil, plus anything that could be placed on top of them. The key point is that the water doesn't flow around these barriers and just comes to a stop. If you want to stop the Asian carp and other invasive species you've got to eliminate their waterway passage.

The Mid-System alternative became the most viable quite quickly. But one of the things we established from the outset was that building barriers wouldn't probably be a very difficult thing to accomplish especially if it was done by the U.S. Army Corps of Engineers. But, there are collateral issues that needed to be dealt with as well.

And, the three big ones are: water transportation; flood control; and, water quality. So, right from the outset, our first objective was to demonstrate the feasibility of physical barriers and separation. However, in order to accomplish that, we needed a way that would actually maintain, or, if possible, enhance transportation, flood control, and water quality. Now, what needs to be recognized is that many other things are going on at the same time, particularly relative to water quality and flood control, including the Deep Tunnel and reservoir projects that began in the early 1970s (and hopefully will be done in 2029). We have integrated our work with the work done by the Metropolitan Water Reclamation District. In addition, we need to push to include and tighten the water quality standards in the Chicago River. This has ultimately been successful, and, in the near term, it will result in MWRD disinfecting waterway discharges. It also may very likely, in the future, result in other kinds of improvements in the water quality. The big problem in relation to water quality and flood control is the extent of combined sewer overflows.

As for transportation, it presents of a different set of challenges. We think that waterborne transportation is a good thing although it has presented some real problems for the Great Lakes in terms of serving as a vector for invasive species to move in over the years. But, from an energy efficiency standpoint, it is a very cost effective means of moving goods. The ships that use the Great Lakes and transport materials from the Great Lakes are much too large to proceed through something like the Illinois and Michigan Canal. If one wants to move materials from the Great Lakes System to the Mississippi River System, then a way to transfer products from ship to barge or barge to ship is necessary. And, while some barges move on the Great Lakes, these are not very weather-worthy types of vessels.

What we are talking about, first, with these various controls is not closing the Chicago Waterway System. The other thing one must do is to place waterborne transportation in context, which is that the goods and materials moving along on barges and through the waterways here are less than 3% of the goods that move through Chicago. Trucks are the biggest movers of goods, with railroads being the second. The largest single commodity in the recent past has been coal, but with the closure of the three coal-fired power plants (Fisk, Crawford and Stateline), the demand for coal in the immediate Chicago area has greatly declined. Overall, allowing barge traffic retains a certain level of importance.

The work that we did basically said that what you have to look at are the materials and how to transfer them from one side of the barriers to the other. This is what we contemplate for the Calumet Harbor area. It will mean using a larger lake ship coming in from Lake Calumet, and having barges on one side and then lifting materials from the ships over the barrier and placed on barges on the other side, or vice versa. Our estimates were that it would add approximately 5% to the time of the shipment on barges and 10% to the cost. Overall, using barges to ship materials is much less expensive than other modes of transportation. Obviously it would reduce the barges' competitive advantage, but it is a very doable thing. We are looking right now at the expenses involved in the creation of such barriers.

As to what the entire proposal would cost, we knew that when we started this project many people weren't even willing to give this serious consideration. In fact, re-reversing the Chicago River was beyond comprehension to many people. Part of my argument for reversal was that if someone was smart enough and able enough to do this in the late 1890s, I would certainly hope that from the standpoint of technology and brain power, we can figure out how to do it today. From a dollar standpoint and putting this in perspective, I believe that the correct figure is that $11-$12 billion was spent on creating the system over the years. So our best estimate for the down river option and the near lake option would be about $9.5 billion, and the mid-system option would be in the $4-$5 billion range, or about half as expensive. In fact, 25 different cities have passed resolutions in their city councils saying that they think that physical separation is the way to go.

The Chicago Area Waterway System, of which the Chicago River is an integral part, as well as the Sanitary and Ship Canal, serves as the link between the Chicago River, the Des Plaines River, and, ultimately, the Illinois River. One really needs to look at the system as a whole in order to be able to effectively block the Asian carp and other invasive species from going in either direction. In the Sanitary and Ship Canal, itself, they haven't found carp although the Asian carp have been found in Lake Calumet. And there continues to be a lot of controversy over the DNA evidence that has been collected by professors at the University of Notre Dame. They believe that there is at least tangible evidence of the presence of Asian carp, even if the carp themselves have not been found. There have been some Asian carp found in lagoons in the Chicago parks, probably thrown into bodies of water by humans. That is another reason why people ask, "Why spend all this money on a barrier when someone can place them in the waterways?" Our answer to this is that the threat is so serious that you have to do everything humanly possible to keep them out. We have learned this the hard way over 100 years and we currently spend about $20-$30 million a year just to keep the sea lampreys from destroying the entire fishery in the Great Lakes. In fact, the kind of damage which the zebra mussels are doing in the Great Lakes is phenomenal, including those found on water intake structures. And, the zebra mussels have served to disrupt the biological balance in the Great Lakes. So, basically, we think that we have made a lot of mistakes in the past by not doing everything possible to keep new invasive species from getting in, and our proposed plan is all about prevention.

Few people talk about the damage done to the Illinois River when the Chicago River was reversed initially. Although the fishery has recovered, much of the waste from the Chicago River continues to harm the Illinois River. There is also the continuing problem of invasive species coming from the Great Lakes. Residents living down-state would like to see a stop to the problem as well. So, there is a much broader constituency concerned about the issue than just residents who live on or near the Great Lakes.

Coming back to the issue of how this would be paid for, we are doing an intensive study on that right now and we are looking at a combination of options. Ultimately, this is a big enough project that federal, state, and local money would need to be involved, and, to the extent that private money can be brought into this, particularly to deal with the transportation side of things that would be appropriate. And, to the extent this can be done in a way that reduces risk, there may be other ways to attract some private money for the project. I think we rate payers of MWRD are going to have to bite the bullet and assume a part of the cost. There would also need to be more reatment of the water, particularly at the North Side O'Brien Plant, just a little north of Rogers Park at McCormick Boulevard and Howard Street.

The Chicago River waterway system would still have the Stickney Plant going toward the Mississippi under the mid-system alternative, and, sooner or later, the nutrients, mainly nitrogen, from the Stickney Plant, get to the Gulf of Mexico. People down the Mississippi don't like the volume of nitrogen that is coming from here, and there is the additional issue from the North Side plant since phosphorus would be flowing into the Great Lakes. But, probably the biggest problem is the continued

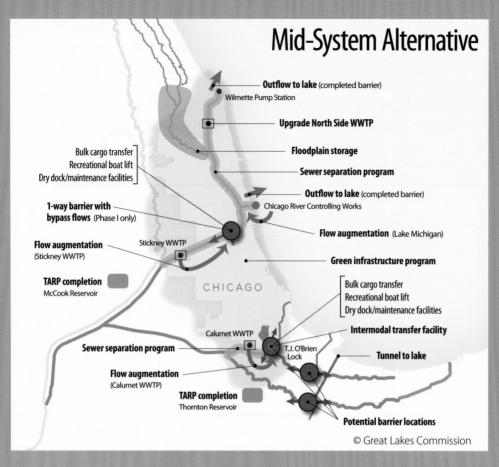

Mid-System Alternative

Outflow to lake (completed barrier)
Wilmette Pump Station

Upgrade North Side WWTP

Floodplain storage

Bulk cargo transfer
Recreational boat lift
Dry dock/maintenance facilities

Sewer separation program

Outflow to lake (completed barrier)
Chicago River Controlling Works

1-way barrier with
bypass flows (Phase I only)

Flow augmentation (Lake Michigan)

Flow augmentation
(Stickney WWTP)

Stickney WWTP

Green infrastructure program

TARP completion
McCook Reservoir

CHICAGO

Bulk cargo transfer
Recreational boat lift
Dry dock/maintenance facilities

Intermodal transfer facility

Calumet WWTP

Sewer separation program

T.J. O'Brien
Lock

Tunnel to lake

Flow augmentation
(Calumet WWTP)

TARP completion
Thornton Reservoir

Potential barrier locations

© Great Lakes Commission

Separation Alternatives

Down River ⬤

Mid-System ⬤

Near Lake ⬤

NORTH SHORE CHANNEL

NORTH BRANCH, CHICAGO RIVER

SOUTH BRANCH, CHICAGO RIVER

CHICAGO RIVER

BUBBLY CREEK

DES PLAINES RIVER

CHICAGO SANITARY AND SHIP CANAL

CHICAGO

LAKE MICHIGAN

LAKE CALUMET

CALUMET RIVER

INDIANA HARBOR

BURNS HARBOR

CAL-SAG CHANNEL

LITTLE CALUMET RIVER

GRAND CALUMET RIVER

INDIANA HARBOR CANAL

ELECTRIC BARRIERS

TO ILLINOIS RIVER

ILLINOIS

INDIANA

HART DITCH

© Great Lakes Commission

Mid-System
Alternative.
Courtesy of the
Great Lakes
Commission.

Separation
Alternatives,
Courtesy of the
Great Lakes
Commission.

Chicago Waterway
Map, Courtesy
of the Great Lakes
Commission.

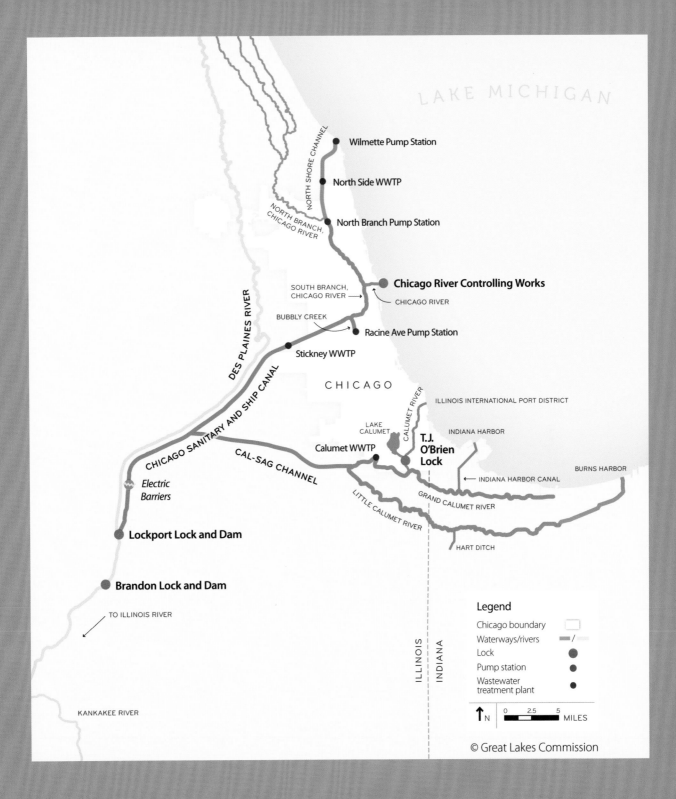

LAKE MICHIGAN

Wilmette Pump Station

North Side WWTP

North Branch Pump Station

NORTH SHORE CHANNEL

NORTH BRANCH,
CHICAGO RIVER

Chicago River Controlling Works

SOUTH BRANCH,
CHICAGO RIVER

CHICAGO RIVER

BUBBLY CREEK

Racine Ave Pump Station

Stickney WWTP

DES PLAINES RIVER

CHICAGO

ILLINOIS INTERNATIONAL PORT DISTRICT

CALUMET RIVER

LAKE
CALUMET

INDIANA HARBOR

Calumet WWTP

T.J.
O'Brien
Lock

CHICAGO SANITARY AND SHIP CANAL

CAL-SAG CHANNEL

INDIANA HARBOR CANAL

BURNS HARBOR

Electric
Barriers

LITTLE CALUMET RIVER

GRAND CALUMET RIVER

Lockport Lock and Dam

HART DITCH

Brandon Lock and Dam

TO ILLINOIS RIVER

ILLINOIS

INDIANA

KANKAKEE RIVER

Legend

Chicago boundary
Waterways/rivers
Lock
Pump station
Wastewater
treatment plant

N

0   2.5   5
MILES

© Great Lakes Commission

combined sewer overflows which will go on until at least 2029 (if TARP is completed by then), and possibly, after that. And there are the increasing dynamics of climate change that are occurring along with more intense precipitation events. MWRD readily acknowledges that it can't handle everything, even with the current reservoirs that will open in 2017. More creative approaches are needed. So, expanded use of green infrastructure is part of the solution, along with possibly other storage devices.

There is much discussion about recreating a new Chicago River. Mayor Emanuel has declared the Chicago River as the new recreational frontier. Jeanne Gang's book and study focus on the aesthetics side of the problem and how to have an attractive barrier, like the one proposed for Bubbly Creek. I think that part of her theory was that it could be used to integrate neighborhoods together, but what I think we are really talking about is totally transforming the attitude of Chicagoans about the Chicago River. Although the river has been focused in its use on commercial transportation and its conveyance of sewage for over 100 years, I think that with the combination of more people on the river and learning about it and the growing importance of the river as it impacts the entire Midwest, there is going to be more pressure for improving water quality.

What can that mean economically for the city? There are many separate but interconnected parts to the proposal along with many financial, political, technical, environmental, and social aspects to these suggested plans of action. The U.S. Army Corps of Engineers is very heavily involved in all of the planning discussions. They are doing the GLMRIS study (Great Lakes, Mississippi River, Inter Basin Study), and part of our reason for proceeding with the barrier proposal is to try to make something happen faster, and to make sure that physical separation received a fair shot. We are hopeful that the best plans will be implemented in the near future.

Kayaks gathered along
south bank of Chicago River with
Marina City in distance.

Margaret Frisbie

The Chicago River system is a critical part of our community. It provides public open space and habitat, and serves as an economic driver for a region. Once a back alleyway, polluted and fenced off, today the river is alive with activity both above and below the water. Despite some peoples' misconceptions, healthy fish populations or wildlife are not mutually exclusive to barges or riverwalks or restaurants or new townhomes or parks or forest preserves—we can have it all.

To me, the Chicago River system clearly has its own right to exist and it must be constantly protected against a variety of threats. To understand the river, I think that it is important to understand where it flows and its various characteristics. It is not just downtown or industrial. It flows through a mosaic of land uses ranging from the urban to suburban to the wild and wooded forest preserves and undeveloped parcels in Cook and Lake Counties. Those places areas are all magical in their own right and they are full of life.

To understand the river system, you have to think about it as a flowing river and not just a series of canals and natural streams with some sections straightened. If you compartmentalize it that way, you are missing "the forest for the trees." For example, the North Shore Channel was dug to create flow in the North Branch that would flush pollution downstream. However, today it is alive with wildlife and was identified by the Illinois Department of Natural Resources as one of the locations in the river system where there is great opportunity to establish quality fish habitat if we can get more dissolved oxygen into the water. The channel already has naturalized banks, ample shade, and nooks and crannies where fish can get away from larger predators. Our goal at Friends of the Chicago River is to ensure that the Illinois Pollution Control Board increases the water quality standards for the aquatic life in the river, which will enforce the need for more dissolved oxygen throughout the system and will directly impact in the North Shore Channel. Whatever its original purpose, that canal has become a key part of our natural landscape.

An ironic twist to the issue of the threat of the Asian carp is that when they poisoned a reach of the Chicago Sanitary and Ship Canal to prevent any potential Asian carp from passing through while repair work was done on the electric barriers, they found no Asian carp. What they discovered instead as they collected dead fish from the water was that populations of different species of fish were reproducing in those waters. That was a big surprise because it was believed by some that there was no possibility that species like catfish were reproducing there. They found young of the year which meant that they were born where they were found since they don't travel too far. That data challenged assumptions and supports the need for new aquatic life standards for the whole river system.

One of the current projects we are working on is dam removal. There are four dams that Friends thinks should be removed to allow fish access to upstream habitat and provide paddlers safe passage downstream. They include Winnetka Road, Tam O'Shanter Golf Course, Chick Evans Golf Course, and the North Branch Dam. Of these dams, only the North Branch at River Park is still really hydrologically significant. It was built by the Metropolitan Water Reclamation District when they constructed the North Shore Channel and changed the hydrology of the river. The new channel was lower than the original river bed and without the addition of the dam water from the Upper North Branch, would have rushed through and drastically eroded the banks. The dam slowed the water.

Friends wants the dams out for two reasons. First, dams are dangerous to paddlers because if paddlers go over them, they can get caught in the back flow that can hold them under the water. Second, the dam prevents fish going upstream. Lots of fish already live in the river and some come in from Lake Michigan. Because of the dams, they cannot go any farther than River Park. Upstream from the dam, as you move further north, there are forest preserves and other places all the way up through Lake County where a lot of restoration work has happened or places that were never that degrade so would provide great habitat. The dams prevent the fish from reaching it. Interestingly, locally we have flatland Midwestern fish, and they are not like salmon in the west that can climb up fish ladders. They need a long, smooth, and steady grade to get over a dam. Rather than try to build long straight fish passage points, Friends wants the dams removed altogether so the fish and paddlers can go through them all. By taking down the four dams, we will be opening up an additional 55 miles of waterways.

There has not been more sewage in the Chicago River system than any other city, but the problem of sewage in our waterways has perhaps lasted longer. All large old cities started with combined sewers, meaning storm pipes and sewer pipes were combined into one system so when it rained, the sewer system was often overwhelmed and sewage was released into our rivers or lakes. In Cook County, the answer to ending combined sewer overflows and flooding was the Tunnel and Reservoir Plan (TARP, aka Deep Tunnel) developed by the Metropolitan Water Reclamation District (MWRD) in the early 1970s. The plan called for 109 miles of tunnel and three reservoirs.

MWRD completed the first tunnel system along the Chicago River in 1986. It was 31 miles long and had a tremendous impact that can be measured by a significant increase in the number of fish and fish species in the river. The first reservoir, which is the Majewski Reservoir, opened in 1998 near O'Hare and has saved the region $250 million in flood damage. The Thornton Reservoir is slated to be completed in 2015 and should virtually eliminate combined sewer overflows in the Calumet system. McCook, which is the last and largest, calculated to hold 10 billion gallons of water, is being completed in two phases. Phase 1's deadline is 2017, and Phase 2 has a targeted completion date of 2029. That deadline is still too long away, and we need to do speed it up and work on eliminating stormwater through green infrastructure at the same time.

Milwaukee has done a really good job at this. They developed the Sweetwater Trust, which is a large partnership of stakeholders who are focused on keeping stormwater out of their combined sewer system. As a result, the number of combined sewer overflows into Milwaukee's rivers and Lake Michigan have dropped dramatically in the last 10 years.

The continually discussed concept of re-reversing the river is a great question with a tricky answer because technically speaking, if done properly, it would be fantastic to have the Chicago River be connected to Lake Michigan. That would require the river water to be as clean as the water in the lake and the water would have to meet the same lake level water quality standards. Clearly, since the lake is clean enough for drinking and swimming in, if the river had the same water quality, it would be very much better than it is now. Also, at present, we also channel clean rainwater into our

Mississippi River Basin

CHICAGO RIVER

LAKE MICHIGAN

DES PLAINES RIVER

APPROXIMATE BASIN DIVIDE

CALUMET RIVER

Great Lakes Basin

© Great Lakes Commission

Near Lake Alternative

NORTH SHORE CHANNEL

NORTH BRANCH, CHICAGO RIVER

SOUTH BRANCH, CHICAGO RIVER

CHICAGO RIVER

BUBBLY CREEK

DES PLAINES RIVER

LAKE MICHIGAN

CHICAGO

CHICAGO SANITARY AND SHIP CANAL

CAL-SAG CHANNEL

LAKE CALUMET

CALUMET RIVER

INDIANA HARBOR

ELECTRIC BARRIERS

LITTLE CALUMET RIVER

BURNS HARBOR

INDIANA HARBOR CANAL

GRAND CALUMET RIVER

TO ILLINOIS RIVER

ILLINOIS | INDIANA

HART DITCH

© Great Lakes Commission

Water Flow in the Chicago Area, circa 1900, Courtesy of the Great Lakes Commission.

Near Lake Alternative, Courtesy of the Great Lakes Commission.

Down River Alternative, Courtesy of the Great Lakes Commission.

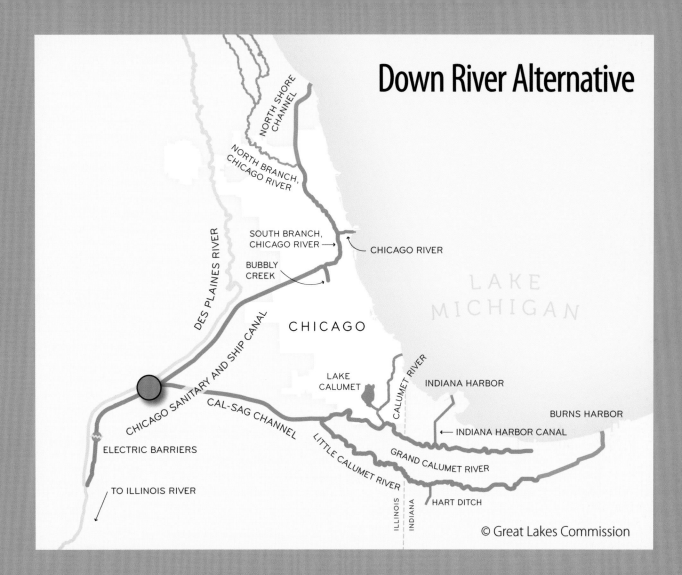

Down River Alternative

NORTH SHORE CHANNEL

NORTH BRANCH, CHICAGO RIVER

SOUTH BRANCH, CHICAGO RIVER

CHICAGO RIVER

BUBBLY CREEK

DES PLAINES RIVER

CHICAGO

LAKE MICHIGAN

LAKE CALUMET

CALUMET RIVER

INDIANA HARBOR

BURNS HARBOR

CHICAGO SANITARY AND SHIP CANAL

CAL-SAG CHANNEL

LITTLE CALUMET RIVER

GRAND CALUMET RIVER

INDIANA HARBOR CANAL

ELECTRIC BARRIERS

TO ILLINOIS RIVER

HART DITCH

ILLINOIS

INDIANA

© Great Lakes Commission

sewer system that once used to recharge our aquifers or flow back into Lake Michigan. All that water is dumped in the river and because of the reversal of it, with any pollutants it picked up along the way, flows downstream and contributes to the dead zone in the Gulf of Mexico.

On the converse side, there is the issue of all of the users and who and what would be blocked by re-reversing the river. Right now, we are advocating an interim solution where there would be some treatment facilities at the Lockport locks that would stop Asian carp from being able to penetrate the river system. (It is important to note that they are not anywhere near it yet.) That would allow us to concentrate and be more thoughtful as to how we solve the larger problem of aquatic invasive species and consider if we might reconnect the river to the lake. If we separate the system at Lockport, for example, then the whole Chicago River system and everybody who lives near and along it would have equal opportunity to access a clean, healthy river.

Another question is whether or not, from an environmental and social justice point of view, how we would be able to guarantee that the water quality is as good at either side of a barrier. Villages and towns along the Cal-Sag System are developing master plans that depend on the use the river because a cleaned up Cal-Sag System is valuable waterfront property. Could they be cut off from clean water?

Finally one more interesting aspect of re-reversing the river is that in every single complete separation scenario proposed so far, nothing can be done until after TARP is finished because there would be nowhere for the river water to go if it cannot flow downstream. Re-reversal before then would mean more flooded basements and combined sewer overflows which is, politically, a nonstarter. So it is quite possible that nothing is going to happen to the river until at least 2029, although it can happen sooner if MWRD moved up the date for the completion of the McCook Reservoir and the region starts doing a better job of managing stormwater.

The conversation about re-reversal is really only happening at all because of the Asian carp threat and aquatic invasive species.

There are many groups and agencies working to solve this complex and ever evolving problem. The U.S. Army Corps of Engineers is conducting the Great Lakes and Mississippi River Interbasin Study (GLMRIS) to identify scenarios for stopping the transfer of aquatic invasives species between the two watersheds. Separation may be among their myriad solutions. President Obama appointed John Goss to develop the Asian Carp Control Strategy Framework to find a solution to stop Asian carp from infiltrating the Great Lakes and, consequently, the rivers and streams that are attached to it. U.S. Fish and Wildlife is also actively studying the problem along with most of the agencies that would have some sort of jurisdiction or interest including a wide variety of associations, mayors, municipalities, and cities like Detroit and Toronto, which are very concerned about the threat of invasive species. There was a two-year study done by the Great Lakes Commission and the Great Lakes and St. Lawrence Seaway Cities Initiative which developed three separation, or re-reversal, scenarios that they released in a report called *Restoring the Natural Divide*. (Of course, the natural divide was about seven feet, so when there was lots of rain, there was a regular flow of water between the systems anyway. Chicago was built here because of that easily exploitable hydrological connection.) In that study, they ruled out many solutions as being impractical or too expensive, and from their research, they recommended a mid-river solution as the best long term approach.

Another concept for dealing with Asian carp which contemplates re-reversal was published by the architect, Jeanne Gang. She focused on reengineering and creating green space around Bubbly Creek. Her project was an academic study and an exercise done by Harvard students whom she was teaching.

I actually participated in a similar class for Phil Enquist from Skidmore, Owings, & Merrill for a similar class project. Enquist, like Gang, taught a studio design class at Harvard University and used the Chicago River as a tool for learning. Their project was to develop ideas for redeveloping an underutilized section of the south branch of the river. The students visited Chicago and toured the river with Friends and Open Lands. To give it context, before they came, they flew me to Harvard where I talked to them for several hours one day. It was so much fun and very interesting because I was able to see, firsthand, those students dealing with the assigned problem and then review their great ideas and solutions for the Chicago River. They were terrifically creative and later developed an exhibit of their ideas that received an award from the American Society of Landscape Architects in 2013.

When I think about the future of the Chicago River, it almost doesn't really matter which way it flows as long as it is a resource for the region and the people and wildlife that share it. For a long time, people accepted the status quo that the Chicago River was polluted and that was the way it was. But that vision was limited and others, including Friends' founders, had the imagination to see past the fences, past the pollutions to see a river that wasn't there. Finally, that vision is shared by almost everybody.

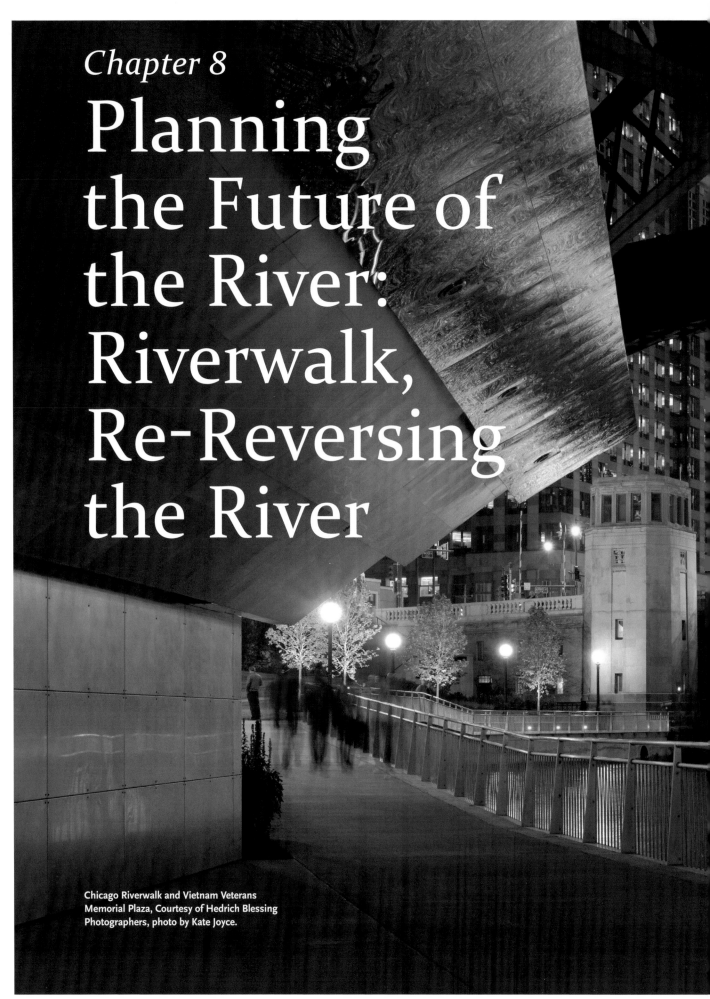

Chapter 8

Planning the Future of the River: Riverwalk, Re-Reversing the River

Chicago Riverwalk and Vietnam Veterans
Memorial Plaza, Courtesy of Hedrich Blessing
Photographers, photo by Kate Joyce.

March 17, 1962 – The city began its tradition of dyeing the Chicago River in the downtown area green, first with fluorescent dye, and later with vegetable dye, in honor of St. Patrick's Day.

1965 – The groundbreaking for the Chicago Botanic Garden began the transformation of the last remaining large piece of the Skokie Marsh.

Late 1960s – A multibillion dollar project called the Tunnel and Reservoir Plan (TARP) was developed and construction began on a deep underground tunnel system to reduce pollution in the Chicago waterways and prevent flooding by capturing billions of gallons of storm water overflows.

1971 – The Union Stock Yards was closed.

1972 – The Federal Clean Water Act passed.

1980–1985 – The O'Hare, Calumet, and Main Stream Deep Tunnel, or Tunnel and Reservoir Project (TARP) tunnels went on-line and the fish population in the Chicago River began to rebound.

April 13, 1992 – Rehabilitation work on the Kinzie Street Bridge crossing the Chicago River required some new dolphin pilings, and unbeknownst to the work crews aboard a barge in the river, one of the pilings on the east bank was driven into an abandoned underground tunnel. Although the dolphin piling did not actually punch through the tunnel wall, it caused such pressure that it cracked the wall and mud began to leak through. This led to the flooding of basements in several Loop office buildings and retail stores as 250 million gallons of water poured in and, in addition, electrical power and natural gas went down or were shut off. It took three days before the flood was cleaned up at an eventual cost to the city some $1.95 billion.

1998 – The U.S. Environmental Protection Agency identified new fish breeds in the river and credited water-quality improvements.

1999 - The development of public space along the Chicago River had been a more complicated task than anticipated over many years, and that land remained generally inaccessible to the public for many years until 1999 when Mayor Richard M. Daley began to implement the Chicago River Corridor Development Plan.

2002 – The Chicago Park District completed a Chicago River Master Plan that laid out strategies for improving open space along the river.

2007–2009 – The Chicago Riverwalk Development Committee was formed to work with the city in developing the walkway known as Riverwalk, and in 2009, the architectural firm of Skidmore, Owings & Merrill created a framework plan that outlined guidelines for the construction of a continuous walkway on both riverbanks along a 1.3 mile long stretch along the river between Lake Street and Lake Michigan. The plan focused on improving access to the riverfront and returning plantings along the river.

Margaret Frisbie

I love the idea of the Chicago Riverwalk, and Friends is in strong support. I am certain that the city is going to make it happen. Under Mayor Emanuel's leadership, the city of Chicago received a low interest, 30 year loan from the U.S. Department of Transportation (USDOT). Phase I of the riverwalk is already complete. Phase II will be the under-bridge connections and build-out from State Street to LaSalle Street. Phase III is from LaSalle Street to Lake Street, and the loan will cover the design and build-out there too. Mayor Daley was fully behind this project, too, and when the city redid the East-West portion of Wacker Drive; they were trying to build this into that construction but just didn't have enough funding at that time. The USDOT loan will now make it possible.

As for whether people will be drawn there, I think that it will be an enormous success once the whole walk is completed. For now, it is crowded during the summertime, but only those areas that have under-bridge connections. In the blocks where you can't get under the bridges, it is a little bit peculiar and people are a bit hesitant to walk in those less populated areas because of homeless people and concern about safety. From State Street eastward to the lake, it is lovely.

I think that our river walk will be better than the one in San Antonio, Texas. The plans are well under way to make it a wonderful linear park alive with activities and restaurants and places for quiet contemplation. Phase II is completely designed and ready to go. Phase III's design is expected to be completed soon and construction within a couple of years as well, although we haven't been given a timeframe for that part of the project. I look forward to the day it is finished.

The new Chicago Riverwalk, Courtesy of
Hedrich Blessing Photographers, photo
by Kate Joyce.

GO REMEMBERS

1969

1970

The Chicago Vietnam Veterans Memorial and Fountain includes the names of Illinois soldiers who died during the war and includes a timeline of significant events during the war. The timeline links each name with a moment in time. Courtesy of Hedrich Blessing Photographers, photo by Kate Joyce.

181

The Riverwalk provides a refuge from
the dense city. Underbridge canopies provide
protection and bounce light into the
dark underside of bridges above, Courtesy
of Hedrich Blessing Photographers, photo
by Kate Joyce.

The Riverwalk educates passersby
with plaques that describe the river ecology.
Courtesy of Hedrich Blessing Photographers,
photo by Kate Joyce.

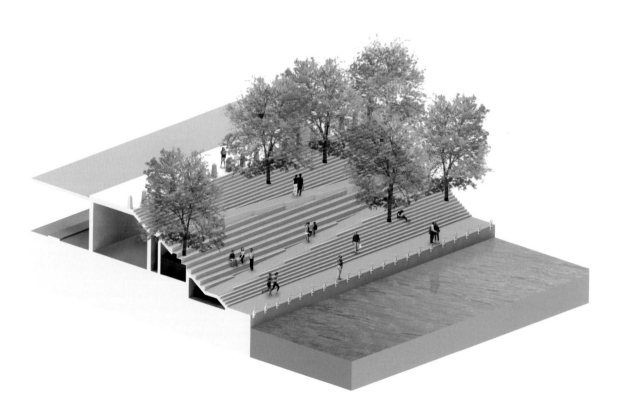

THE RIVERWALK PLAN

BOARDWALK · JETTY · SWIMMING HOLE · RIVER THEATER · COVE · MARINA PLAZA

FRANKLIN ST · WELLS ST · LASALLE ST · CLARK ST · DEARBORN ST · STATE ST

WACKER DRIVE

The new extension of the Chicago Riverwalk. Courtesy of the Riverwalk Team, Phase II, the Chicago Department of Transportation (Michelle Woods, Project Manager), Sasaki Associates, and Ross Barney Architects.

Various sites as part of the new extension of the Chicago Riverwalk and the Riverwalk Plan. Courtesy of the Riverwalk Team, Phase II, the Chicago Department of Transportation (Michelle Woods, Project Manager), Sasaki Associates, and Ross Barney Architects.

The Chicago Vietnam Veterans Memorial and Fountain is both educational and symbolic. Courtesy of Hedrich Blessing Photographers, photo by Kate Joyce.

The Michigan Avenue Bridge and the
new extension of the Chicago Riverwalk.
Courtesy of Hedrich Blessing
Photographers, photo by Kate Joyce.

In addition, credit for the Chicago Riverwalk belongs to the Chicago Department of Transportation, Michelle Woods, Project Manager, Sasaki Associates(prime, Landscape Architect, Civil), Ross Barney Architects (Architecture), Schuler Shook (Lighting), Infrastructure Engineers (Civil Engineering), Benesch (Structural and Marine Engineering), Rubinos and Mesia Engineers (Structural Engineer), Delta Engineering Group (MEP Engineering), Jacobs/Ryan Associates (Landscape Architect), Moffat+Nichol (Boating/Waterway Consultant), Conservation Design Forum (River Hydraulics/Sustainable Landscape), Dynasty Group (Surveyor), GeoServices (Geotechnical), and David Solzman (Historian).